Celtic Journeys

A Traveler's Memoir

Expanded Edition of *My Celtic Journey*

Gerald Herter

Published in the United States of America

Leananshee Press

ISBN 979-8-9850512-0-9
ISBN 979-8-9850512-1-6 (ebook)

www.gaeltales.com

Cover Design by Zizi Iryaspraha Subiyarta

To Lori, my loving companion on life's travels

For a free bonus story, sign up for the Reader List at www.gaeltales.com.

Contents

Preface

I am 25% Scotch Irish. Yet it was my wife, Lori, who first developed a passion for Ireland and all of Celtic Britain. She has no Irish bloodline, being equally Swedish and Czech. However, from her first encounter with the lyrically beguiling voices of the Irish Tenors, she was hooked. The evocative scenes, sounds and senses of the Celtic people and places depicted in their music, sent her yearning to experience this land of magical legends and stirring history. Once there, the feelings she felt for this special world soon captured my heart as well.

So began a continuing love affair with the Celtic world. Whether following the Irish Tenors as they toured, or traveling to the storied places of song, our love for this ancient land and the modern day keepers of the ageless traditions grew. The stories on these pages are a sampling of our ongoing journey.

Preface to the Expanded Edition

Six years ago, the First Edition of My Celtic Journey appeared. Since then, further travels with Celtic connections beckoned us. Along with returns to Ireland and Wales, Cornwall joined the list of Celtic countries visited. Also, Celtic influences in Canada, Iceland and South Africa broadened the scope of coverage. Nine new stories recount these new adventures in the Expanded Edition, along with a selection of photographs from all twenty-four stories.

Part 1 - Ireland

New Year's Eve in Dublin

Anthony Kearns

Chapter 1

Finding the Tenor of Ireland

*Planes, trains, and automobiles track a
holiday concert tour*

Little did I know when my wife, Lori, and I
attended our first Irish Tenors concert at the Greek
Theatre in Los Angeles, that one day we would follow
them across Ireland. But here we were several years
later, as our Aer Lingus flight landed in Shannon on
December 23rd.

Lori fell in love with the Irish Tenors from the
start. From their lyrical music, she also soon fell in love
with Ireland. She longed to experience the places that
the beautiful and haunting songs so richly brought to
life. When the Irish Tenors announced a holiday
concert tour in Ireland, how could I say no?

But first there was Christmas at the welcoming
Park Hotel in quaint Kenmare. Christmas Eve found us
washing down mince pies with warm mead at
midnight, following a brisk walk back from the village
church. We woke in the morning to a light snow.
Before we knew it, Santa Claus arrived, doling out
presents to the children. A scavenger hunt, black tie
dinner and Boxing Day walk completed the festivities
and put us in the spirit for our cross country adventure.

The first concert was December 28 at the Irish
National Event Center (INEC) in nearby Killarney,
known more for beautiful lakes and the timeless
"Christmas in Killarney." Seeing the venue filled with

delighted fans, we knew the concert tour would be a success. The mix of Irish folk songs, along with sacred and holiday selections, was enchanting, especially here in the country that inspired them.

Though awed at the dazzling performance, Lori's heart sank when a bout with the flu prevented her favorite, Anthony Kearns, from performing his solos. Heroically, Kearns still sang the group numbers with surprising gusto, leaving a fellow tenor to remark "I swear that boy has two sets of lungs."

Early the next morning we boarded a train heading north to Belfast for that night's concert. While crossing the country at high speed, we were mesmerized by the passing radiance of the "Forty Shades of Green" that Johnny Cash's classic song so rightly celebrated. By late afternoon, our journey was complete as we rolled into the historic capital of Northern Ireland, and made our way to the Odyssey Arena.

Several times larger than the INEC, the Odyssey had us missing the intimacy of Killarney. Those feelings were quickly dispelled, however, when the Irish Tenors continued to spin their magic. Songs like the "Courtin' Medley" brought laughter as the "boys" teased each other while prancing around to the music. Alas, Anthony's flu lingered on, leaving Lori still longing to hear his rich solo voice.

In the morning, with two days before the New Year's Eve concert in Dublin, we hired a rental car and spent a night at coastal Annalong, nestled beneath the "Mountains of Mourne," as they "swept down to the sea," as described in the song.

From there, an easy drive brought us to Dublin's Point Theatre (now the O_2) for the grand finale. A cold wintry wind off the River Liffey greeted us as we entered the majestic hall. Though we were hearing the Irish Tenors for the third time in four nights, the captivating charm of their lush, soaring voices had not worn off. The poignant "Silent Night" conjured up nostalgic memories. Lori finally was able to smile wholeheartedly when Anthony Kearns, his illness now behind him, rose to give an emotionally heartfelt performance of "If You Can Help Somebody." Then as the concert drew to a close, the bells rang out at midnight. Everyone, the Irish Tenors included, crossed arms and held hands with their neighbor as all sang "Auld Lang Syne."

Park Hotel Kenmare

Downtown Kenmare and Holy Cross Church

Chapter 2

Christmas in Kenmare

An Irish blessing triumphs over the impossible

Note: Three years after returning home from the Ireland recounted in Chapter 1, I shared another aspect of that journey with the congregation at my church, as part of a year-end drive to balance the church's budget.

Good Morning!

I feel like a waiter today.

You know when you've been to a fine restaurant and just finished a sumptuous meal. You feel filled and satisfied. Then the waiter appears with the bill and you're shocked at how much it cost.

We've just had a glorious advent season. The pastors, choir and staff have all provided us with wonderful helpings of messages, music and programs to commemorate the birth of our Lord. We are truly filled and satisfied.

Now along comes the waiter, the church Treasurer. You've gotten your money's worth. Now it's time to pay the bill. Year end is always a challenging time for churches with regards to finances. This year is no exception for our church. In fact, we are some $50,000 short of balancing the budget. A seemingly impossible task with only a couple days left.

As I pondered this impossible situation, I was reminded of a Christmas three years ago that Lori and I spent in Ireland. There we saw first hand the results of an impossible task that was accomplished by people trusting in God and at the same time rolling up their sleeves and doing the hard work necessary to fulfill God's will.

We arrived on Christmas Eve at a small country hotel at the edge of the village of Kenmare, in County Kerry, not far from Killarney. That evening, we learned that the protestant Church of Ireland was just a short walk from the hotel, and had a service at 11 PM. Also, just a little further at the other end of the village, Holy Cross Catholic church would be celebrating midnight mass.

So we bundled up and headed out into the cold winter night. It was below freezing. We got to the church and settled into a pew and discovered there was no heat in the church. We don't know how spoiled we are in California. But we may find out if we don't get the budget balanced! However, that's not the point of my story.

The minister started the service. A couple minutes later, the door opened. A man in clerical garb walked right down the center aisle and up to the pulpit. He turned to the congregation and said "I'm Father Murphy from Holy Cross Catholic Church. This is the first time I have been in this pulpit. I bring you greetings from your brothers and sisters in Christ at Holy Cross. And if you'll allow me, I would like to offer a blessing and prayer for you. He then proceeded to give the most wonderful prayer of hope, peace and love. Then he and the minister embraced and he walked out. When he continued the service, the minister said "After we're done, I am going to walk over to Holy Cross and bring our greetings to them.

This was a poignant moment for Lori and me. We knew that only a few short years earlier, the Catholics and Protestants in Northern Ireland had been killing each other. Terrorist bombs were frequent. British soldiers shot rebels and got shot. This simple gesture on Christmas Eve in a small village church spoke volumes of how far all the Irish people had come in overcoming centuries of hatred and animosity.

A few days later we took a train to Belfast. The following day we rented a car to drive to Dublin. On the way, we crossed the border between Northern Ireland and the Republic of Ireland at 65 miles per hr (100km/hr). We hardly knew we had just passed from one sovereign country to another. Once again we were struck by how the Irish had overcome a seemingly impossible task and were now more closely integrated than ever. Through hard work and persistent trust in God, the impossible was accomplished.

There are many impossible situations in our world today. I don't pretend to have answers for them. But we have our own difficult challenge right here, attempting to bridge the gap in our budget. Let's all of us take some time in the next few days to be prayerful and ask God how we individually might play a part in overcoming our impossible task.

In closing, on that New Year's Eve, three years ago, as we listened to the Irish Tenors in concert in Dublin, at the midnight hour, the audience stood and took each other's hands in the Irish traditional way. And as they rung in the New Year, the words of one of the songs from the evening stuck with me. Now I won't do the impossible and sing it for you. But here are some of the words: To Do Thy Will.

To do your will, is my desire,
To live in you, Lord is my life.
To spread your love, through all the earth,
To find in you, the joy of life.

All of my days, I sing your praise,
Through all my nights, you are my life.
You will shine forth, through all my years,
And joyously will bring me home.

I search this world so restlessly,
Seeking a home from hate and strife.
I found in you, the strength to see,
The meaning of this troubled life.

And so my God, I give to you,
These raining words these restless rhymes,
And take my life as a tribute of,
Your endless love for all mankind.

Bantry House

Poulnabrone Dolmen

Chapter 3

In Search of Gloccamorra

Finding the Ireland of song

You might not expect a dozen Americans to be in the audience at the Grand Hotel in Wicklow, Ireland for the concert that opened the annual Wicklow Regatta Festival in July. Their interest had nothing to do with boats or the aquatic activities in this coastal town just a short drive south of Dublin. No, they were there to hear Anthony Kearns, of The Irish Tenors fame, sing on his home turf, perhaps for the last time in such an intimate, up close setting.

Indeed, in his earlier years, Kearns had worked at the Grand Hotel as night porter, among other duties. Late that evening, after the concert, he reflected that he "did not mind one bit" the hard work in that formative time in his life. Nowadays, he is more likely seen at venues like Carnegie Hall, Radio City Music Hall or on PBS, along with Finbar Wright and Ronan Tynan, as The Irish Tenors.

Over the past year and a half, my wife, Lori, had lost her heart to The Irish Tenors and the rich, poignant music of the Emerald Isle. "How Are Things in Gloccamorra?" is Hollywood's idea of Ireland. We wanted to see the real thing based on authentic Irish songs. So here we were at the start of a two week pilgrimage to places immortalized in songs like "Boolavogue," "The Fields of Athenry," "Bantry Bay," "Galway Bay" and "Slievenamon." We'd planned our trip by the songs listed on the covers of the Irish Tenors' albums.

The next morning we were still moved by Kearns powerful, yet sensitive interpretations. Lori was savoring the memory of his expressive voice as we drove across the midsection of Ireland enroute to Galway on the west coast.

In the afternoon, we relived the lament of a peasant couple long ago as we approached the town from the popular Irish song, "Fields of Athenry." Athenry is a small medieval town with well preserved gray ruins of King John's Castle, a Dominican abbey, a landmark spired church and fourteenth century town walls that are among the best remaining in Ireland. The town is surrounded by the lush low lying fields depicted in the song, some planted in potatoes. The song harkens back to the days of famine in the mid-1800's, when an impoverished family struggled to survive. The desperate father "stole Trevelyn's corn," so his child might "see the morn." But he's caught and sentenced to a prison ship bound for Botany Bay in Australia. The ship, most likely, embarked from nearby Galway Bay, our destination for the night.

Before leaving Athenry though, we could not help but peruse the offerings of a local entrepreneur who had opened the "Fields of Athenry Gift Shop," the only visible sign of commercialism in this otherwise unpretentious, but fascinating historical town. Lori settled on a poster with the words from the song surrounded by copies of paintings portraying scenes from this sad time.

Later that afternoon, we arrived at the Connemara Coast Hotel, which is right on the bay, six miles west of Galway. The guidebook mentioned this hotel as the place to stay to "watch the sun go down on Galway Bay," as the song, "Galway Bay," relates.

A modern seaside hotel elegantly decorated, the Connemara Coast has rooms on several stories, all with a bay view. We walked down to the boulder covered shore, hopping on barnacle covered rocks and around stream fed tide pools. The bright sun glistened on the waves, while we gazed across the wide bay at the mountains of County Clare in the distance and further out to the Aran Islands, looming on the horizon. Along with our dinner of salmon and lemon sole that evening, we watched the sun descend to the sounds of "Galway Bay" and other traditional Irish melodies romantically rendered on the piano.

The morning brought us back to the reality of Ireland as we woke to gray and rainy skies. Our day's journey along the dramatic Galway Bay coastline and through the majestic Connemara National Park mountains was experienced wearing sweaters and ponchos. Even so, the downpours could not lessen the charm of stately Kylemore Abbey, nestled serenely on the misty shores of Kylemore Lough. Home of the Benedictine Order of nuns, the abbey also runs an international girls' school.

The next day the skies cleared and we sang verses of the "Darling Girl From Clare" while driving through the county of that name, south of Galway. We noted there was no shortage of pretty, young colleens that could fit the description of the girl in the song. One of them guided us through Ailwee Cave, the only public cavern of many that dot the limestone studded area known as the Burren. The thirty-five minute tour covered traditional cave formations, like stalactites and stalagmites, as well as hibernation chambers for now extinct bears.

Not found in the cave, but nearby, were dolmens, mysterious tombs of early inhabitants of the land from 2,500 to 2,000 BC. Though tiny compared to Egypt's pyramids, the dolmen's function is similar, and the capstone, which can weigh ten to forty-five tons, required a highly structured society years to put in place. From a distance, the dolmen's appearance reminded me of the symbol π.

A visit to this part of Ireland is not complete without a stop at the dramatic Cliffs of Moher, the sheer stretch of 760 foot high limestone walls that border the Atlantic Ocean. A musician with a button accordion filled the air along the cliffside pathway with the lilting namesake melody of the landmark. Lori dropped a coin in his hat in appreciation. However, we were constantly aware here, as later at the lakes of Killarney, of the heightened impact tourism has made since our visit twenty years earlier. The lineup of tour buses at the Cliffs seemed endless, while what used to be quaint, sleepy Muckross House in Killarney, has become a major site with a separate, modern restaurant and shop.

We continued on to the more peaceful Bantry Bay, in the southwest corner of Ireland. Bantry House, in the White family for over 260 years, sits grandly on a terrace with a commanding view of the tranquil bay. We sat alone there contemplating, recalling the words to its namesake song, "all peacefully from Bantry Bay." It was hard to imagine that this placid setting once played a tragic role in the long struggle for

Ireland's independence. In the 1790's, the Irish staged a revolution similar to America's, to gain freedom from England. Like the Americans, the Irish enlisted the help of the French. Here, in 1796, an armada of 43 French ships approached, bringing thousands of troops to support the Irish cause. As they entered Bantry Bay, a hurricane struck, causing many of the ships to be lost. The rest could not land, leaving the Irish to fight on their own.

I asked our host at Bantry House, Egerton Shelswell-White, about the ill-fated invasion. He confirmed that his ancestor, Richard White, received the title, Earl of Bantry, for his efforts to defend against the French, had they landed. He diligently organized local forces around the Bay. Though the weather did the job for them, White was recognized for his gallant actions. In one of Bantry House's buildings, an informative multimedia exhibit describes in pictures, posters and audio, the events of that time. Also displayed are the excavation efforts to salvage one of the French ships that sunk and has lain at the bottom of the Bay for 200 years.

Several days later, outside of Enniscorthy in County Wexford, we would again encounter the saga of the 1798 revolution. To get there however, we first needed to pass through Kinsale on the southern coast, often mentioned as Ireland's prettiest city on the sea. Kinsale is also Irish Tenor Finbar Wright's home town.

Ringing a small bay filled with fishing and pleasure boats, the picturesque port gains a fairy tale appearance when viewed from Charles Fort, an imposing historic defensive structure far out on a point of land. Though effective in fending off attacks by sea, the fort proved vulnerable by land, as the British demonstrated in the 1601 Battle of Kinsale.

A further stop was made at inland Cashel, so that we could drive around the nearby mountain for which the song, "Slievenamon," was named. The song relates the longing of a distant countryman for "the sweet maiden I met in the valley of Slievenamon." Typical of most mountains in Ireland, Slievenamon would rank as a foothill next to America's Rockies. But the checkerboard effect of the light green fields bordered by the dark green hedges and trees covering the gentle slopes gives a special charm to the landscape that is distinctly Irish.

Cashel is known for the Rock of Cashel, the lofty ruins of a centuries old ecclesiastical complex atop a several hundred foot high outcropping on one edge of the city. Prior to 1101, the Rock served as a fortress for the kings of Munster as far back as the fourth century. We passed the night at the Cashel Palace Hotel, the bygone residence of the archbishop, and walked the former cleric's private pathway to the top of the Rock. Sleeping was a challenge as this Friday night was the start of a Bank Holiday weekend. The singing and laughter from nearby pubs carried on to the wee hours.

Finally on Saturday, we arrived in County Wexford in the Southeast. On this bright, sunny day, we stood atop Vinegar Hill, with dramatic views in all directions of the multihued countryside and the town of Enniscorthy close at hand below. According to the song "Boolavogue," it was here the "boys of Wexford" in 1798 staged a courageous but futile battle against the British that turned the tide in their fight for independence. We passed through the tiny town of

Boolavogue and drove a country road to stand in Father Murphy's cottage. As the haunting words of the song relate, Father Murphy led the freedom fighters in a few early victories before being beaten back. When he was captured, they "burned his body on the rack."

While Lori and I reflected back two hundred years, we were eerily reminded of how closely the Irish struggle for freedom resembled our own in America. We were fortunate to win our independence, however, while the Irish would have to wait another one hundred-twenty-five years.

After a few days relaxing amongst the beauty of the Wicklow Mountains National Park, we proceeded to Dublin for the final chapter in the Republic of Ireland's long, hard road to freedom. At Old Kilmainham Gaol on Dublin's west side, Ireland's vanquished patriots were imprisoned and executed from 1798 until 1923. A museum now, the jail is a solemn, silent monument whose dark, grim cells are still damp with the memories of those who gave their all for the homeland.

An especially touching and painful account from the 1916 Rising is remembered in the tragic love song "Grace." Joseph Plunkett was one of the leaders of a rebellion in Dublin that like the previous ones, failed. Though unsuccessful, the 1916 Rising did lay the groundwork for efforts that ultimately led to Ireland's independence in 1923. Captured, Plunkett, along with the other rebel leaders, was sentenced to death. Four hours before being shot in front of a firing squad, Plunkett was married in the prison chapel to his sweetheart, Grace Gifford. His love letter to her and her journal are displayed in the museum.

In contrast to the difficult days early in the past century, we could sense that Ireland's capital had entered the twenty-first century with the confidence and pride that a new found economic prosperity has brought. Still, Dublin is a city rich in history.

Founded by Vikings in 841, Dublin's numerous traditions are evident, among them the brewery for Guinness Stout, and the uniquely Irish sport of hurling, reminiscent of field hockey. The revered eighth century Book of Kells, housed at Trinity College, personifies the crucial role played by Irish monasteries in preserving the tenets and scriptures of Christianity from extinction, between Roman and medieval times. The Book is an ornately decorated rendition of the gospels. On a lighter note, walking along the shopping district of Grafton Street, a statue of lovely Molly Malone offers "cockles and mussels alive alive-o."

Our final night, as we contemplated all we had experienced, we realized we had found the mythical Gloccamorra in the spirit of the land, her people and their timeless songs.

Rossnaree House

Newgrange

Chapter 4

Rossnaree

A ford at the crossroads of Ireland's history

"William of Orange's troops crossed the Boyne right over there," Aisling Law observed, pointing left toward the riverbank, just below the sitting room window we peered from at Rossnaree. We were having a glass of wine with members of Aisling's family before dinner at her home, named after the spot where a key ford helped win the Battle of the Boyne in 1690.

Gazing across the river in the fading sunlight, we watched as growing shadows set apart the megalithic green mounds of Newgrange and Knowth, overlooking lush fields where sheep and cattle grazed. "What an appealing way to take in the breadth of Irish history, all in one spot," I thought. A first timer arriving at the airport in Dublin has only to drive a half hour north to reach this inviting and tranquil country house from where the whole essence of Ireland's past can be absorbed.

Sites within view or just a few miles away present a veritable chronology of the Emerald Island's heritage: prehistoric passage tombs; Tara, the seat of the High Kings from the early Iron Age to the twelfth century; Slane, the hill where St. Patrick challenged the High Kings in 433; the Williamite's decisive Boyne battlefield; a resting place of fallen patriots in the failed 1798 fight for independence; and the Earl of Drogheda homestead at Rossnaree, originally built upon in 1720, added to in 1855, and acquired by the family of Aisling's husband in 1925, not long after the Irish Free State was launched in nearby Dublin.

My wife, Lori, and I had arrived at Rossnaree late in the morning the day before, after a long flight from Los Angeles. Turning in at the gate, a couple miles from Slane, we drove past the old gatehouse cottage, and up the winding wooded drive to the mauve colored Italianate style manor house.

Our rental car glistened from scattered showers, reflecting the patchy May sunshine, as we stepped out to a rousing welcome from rambunctious Rocky, the resident Collie, and Dagda, the regal Irish Wolfhound. Their wagging tales signaled approval to Aisling, who was crossing the wide lawn from the walled gardens to greet us. "I remember you," she smiled giving us warm hugs, recalling our visit eighteen months earlier. "The William Morris Room you reserved is not made up yet. You can have the Bird Room if you like." The Bird Room was bright and airy, the walls adorned with colorful birds painted by her nephew, artist Sam Horler. However, the William Morris Room was spacious, with broad bay windows looking out over the historic grassy meadows. "There's no hurry. We'll drive over to Newgrange for lunch and a visit," I suggested.

The Bru na Boinne ("Palace of the Boyne," the Celtic name for Newgrange) Interpretative Center is just two miles from Rossnaree. But with jetlag starting to set in, we knew we would need to be extra cautious tackling the Irish roads. The drive from the airport had not been overly treacherous. Even though driving is on the left hand side of the road, most of the route is on a multilane Motorway with ample signs and ramps to ease the way. However, once off the Motorway, the rest of the Irish highway system can make for a harrowing experience for the unsuspecting visitor. Often the two lane roads are more like a lane and a half by American standards, while some country lanes are only wide enough for one vehicle with an occasional widening where two oncoming vehicles somehow squeeze by each other. That doesn't stop the locals from driving at breakneck speeds, tailgating as they go. Large trucks and buses use the same roads and habits as well, such that a newcomer tends to cringe at each of the frequent curves, hoping a semi isn't barreling along just around the bend.

Arriving without incident, we parked and proceeded along the atrium covered walkway that winds through a wooded area toward the Visitor Center. The Irish have done well in designing the Newgrange experience for visitors, retaining the ancient character of the surroundings, while catering to creature comforts in the modern Center. The actual sites of the Newgrange and Knowth passage tombs are a mile or two away across the Boyne, and accessible only by a special bus. Just past the Center entrance, guides stand ready to take signups for the tours. Then at the appointed time, they direct each group to a path out the back that takes them over a footbridge crossing the river and on to the waiting busses. The tour to each monument complex takes about 75 minutes including the bus ride.

Newgrange is the largest and best preserved of the many passage tombs that are scattered across Ireland. Built 500 years before the pyramids of Egypt, the circular structure is 250 feet in diameter and 40 feet tall, with a 60 foot tunnel leading to the 20 foot high waterproof burial chamber topped by a 6 ton capstone. Traversing the narrow passage, the modern day seeker walks the way of the ancient ones. The architectural soundness of the large interlaced slabs of rock amazes. But to experience a full sense of the intellect and spirituality of these mysterious people requires a winning lottery ticket for the right to be present at the winter solstice. Then, at the break of day, the sun's rays penetrate precisely through the entire length of the long passage, illuminating the burial chamber with golden hues for a moment, uniquely on that one day of the year. Since only twenty visitors can fit in the chamber, the lucky few are an exclusive group.

Lori and I had toured both Newgrange and the similar Knowth on previous trips, so we opted instead to stop in the tearoom for a lunch of chicken curry before returning to Rossnaree for an afternoon nap. Dinner that night was in Slane, two miles in the opposite direction of Newgrange. Aisling recommended the converted Old Post Office in the center of the small village, where the friendly proprietor served us generous helpings of roast duck and chicken schnitzel, accompanied of course with a creamy-headed pint of Guinness.

Back at Rossnaree, we took one last look at Newgrange in the moonlight, before retiring to an inviting four poster bed.

At breakfast, Aisling entered the dining room with a warm "Good Morning" as she set hot bowls in front of us. "While you eat your porridge, I'll go get the eggs from under the hens." Along with the hens, she has a couple horses, a mule, the two dogs, several cats including one named Champagne, and a large friendly pig called Celeste.

Aisling exudes an engaging love and energetic commitment for all that Rossnaree stands for. At the same time, she makes her guests feel like old friends from the moment she meets them, making them her complete focus. At one point while intently sharing stories, her eyes widened suddenly as she exclaimed "Oh, your eggs!!" She rushed to the kitchen to rescue our breakfast cooking there.

Having renewed our acquaintance with prehistoric Newgrange the day before, we were ready to move up to a period where recorded history and Celtic mythology entwined. Along with the chance to learn more about the Irish High Kings, Lori also had an interest in the lore of mythical creatures for which the country is so well known. The Hill of Tara lies about 12 miles south of Rossnaree. On arriving beside Tara's gently sloping grass covered mounds, we were greeted by Michael Maguire, as he busily tidied up displays of souvenirs in his shop. When Lori remarked that his shop was mentioned in a book she had, *Mysterious World Ireland* (Mysterious World Press, 2006), Michael stopped his work abruptly and joined us in a walk to our car to retrieve the guide. His two year old dog, a boxer named Ruby, scampered playfully by his side. Pleased by the favorable reference he read in the book, Michael took a moment to tell us his family had lived at the historic site for seven generations. Then glancing at the untended shop, he turned to go back, declaring "If I stand more than ten minutes, I'll end up there in the churchyard," pointing to the nearby array of tombstones where his ancestors are buried. They lie next to an old church that serves as an interpretive center.

Back at the shop, Lori asked him for directions to a "fairy tree" she had heard about. Fairy trees were thought to be an entry point to the Celtic Otherworld. Referring to a wall map, Michael directed us to the location. We tramped across the berm ringed meadow to a lone white hawthorn covered with blossoms. True to tradition, the tree had ribbons and other bits of clothing tied to branches, as well as coins wedged into crevices. These are meant to bring good luck. Lori acted out another tradition, circling around the tree three times clockwise, or "sunwise", thought to draw down the sun's healing power.

We returned to the mounded section of the plain and stood next to the *Lialh Fail,* "stone of destiny." Also known as the Coronation Stone, the four foot high obelisk is the only obvious structure remaining of the royal seat of the High Kings. Thought to be the political and spiritual center of Ireland for hundreds of years until the twelfth century, Tara's manmade dwellings have long since decomposed. Still, the historic importance of Tara to the Irish is evoked in diverse ways, even including the naming of the mansion in *Gone With the Wind* by its Irish owner.

Rossnaree also figures in the legends of Tara, relating to the High King Cormac Mac Airt. Well regarded in the third century, he was considered by some historians to have paved the way for early Christianity to make inroads on the dominant pagan Druidism. In that regard, Irish poet Samuel Ferguson in his nineteenth century poem, "The burial of King

Cormac," immortalized the king's wish that he not be buried at Bru na Boinne, the traditional burial place of the High Kings, but at Rossnaree:

> *Spread not the beds of Brugh for me*
> *When restless death-bed's use is done:*
> *But bury me at Rossnaree*
> *And face me to the rising sun.*
> *For all the kings who lie in Brugh*
> *Put trust in gods of wood and stone;*
> *And 'twas at Ross that first I knew*
> *One, Unseen, who is god alone.*

After a lunch of vegetable soup and brown bread in Maguire's Cafe, Lori had one more question for Michael. She wanted to learn about another mythical creature she was planning to use in a story she was writing. The Leanan Sidhe (pronounced lenanshee) is a beautiful female who causes a man to fall hopelessly in love with her, and then abandons him. Michael pointed her to a small, worn building next door where Michael Slavin runs the Old Book Shop.

We entered the stone shop which appeared as ancient as many of the ruins we had visited. There an older man was bent over a book on a table covered with dozens of volumes. "Michael sent us to you," Lori greeted him. "You've met Michael Maguire?" he responded. "We're both Michael. He's the more important Michael. He says I'm the more important. I say he is. So we argue over nothing." "That's a nice argument to have," Lori replied. There is substance to his remarks, though. While he pointed out that Maguire's family has been here for 250 years, we discovered that Slavin himself has published four books on the history and sights of Tara and Ireland. He showed Lori an old book of Irish lore, and then we bid farewell after buying a signed copy of his *The Book of Tara*.

Surveying the countryside on the way out, we spotted a tower on a distant hill that reminded us of another key moment in Ireland's religious past. An annual event on the Hill of Tara in early times celebrated the awakening of summer. No fire was to be lit in all of Ireland that night until the High King at Tara lit the celebratory fire. However, in 433 on that very night, St. Patrick lit a Paschal fire on the Hill of Slane, in full view of Tara and in defiance of the High King. That extraordinary event further symbolized the decline of paganism as the forces of Christianity flourished.

Of course we had to experience the view looking back from the Hill of Slane, so we drove the ten miles separating the two landmarks. There we found a statue of St. Patrick standing in front of ruins of an ancient church and graveyard. Across Ireland, many churches, wells and other notable places bear the name of Ireland's patron saint. Patrick was actually of English origin, first introduced to fifth century Ireland as a slave of Irish raiders. Escaping back to England after six years, he entered the church from where, after a time, he was called once again to Ireland on a lifelong mission.

We arrived back at Rossnaree that afternoon with a new perspective of the location's historical prominence. Sam restored our thoughts to the present, as he approached with a request from Aisling that we join the family for dinner. Delighted at the offer, we freshened up and then went down to the sitting room, where they were all gathered with glasses of wine. After sharing some of the early stories of Rossnaree, Aisling invited us into the dining room across the hall.

Ancestors of the Law family peered down on us from paintings that covered the walls like a series of old masters. I was seated between Judy Law, Aisling's mother-in-law, and Emilia Law, a very pregnant daughter-in-law. Lori sat opposite, between Simon, Emilia's father, and nephew Sam.

Judy, a tall, smartly dressed octogenarian born in England, asked my profession. "I'm an accountant," I replied. "O how boring," she sighed dismissively, flicking the ash off her cigarette. Startled by her reaction I tactfully countered that my job provided splendid opportunities to observe how companies made various products. She wasn't convinced. "Sounds dreadful!" she frowned, turning away. Only later did Aisling confide that Judy's dour sense of humor was not to be taken seriously. To give us a feel for the range of the colorful lady's eccentricities, Aisling related a time during the twenty-five year span when Judy ran the household. She was out trimming trees in the yard wearing only the skimpiest of bikinis. The very sight of her caused the local priest riding by to fall right off his bicycle from the shock.

Retiring to bed after a delicious dinner seasoned with more spirited conversation, Lori and I marveled at how the family history proved to be such a fitting complement to the multi-layered lore of the land. Aisling's late husband, Robert Law, hailed from a tradition of military service. He spent eight years in

Uganda with his new wife, Aisling, where he employed his legal training, helping the country draft a new constitution. Robert's mother, the unpredictable Judy, was a descendent of the artist, William Hogarth.

Aisling is the great granddaughter of Maud Gonne, well known in Ireland's troubled history as a fervent nationalist spokeswoman for Irish independence, as well as muse and love interest of poet William Butler Yeats. Shortly after the United States of America won independence from England, the Irish tried to follow suit. Sadly, the rebellion was put down in 1798, leaving more than a century to pass before freedom fighters supported by Gonne finally succeeded in the 1920's. We had been reminded of the ill-fated struggle of 1798, while at the Hill of Tara. There 400 Irish rebels lost their lives in a tragic battle with British forces. Michael Maguire had recounted how even in recent years nearby farmers were still finding bones from the unfortunate soldiers.

The unassuming Aisling's genes are even further steeped in cultural riches. Her grandfather, Francis Stuart, was a noted Irish writer, while her mother, Imogen Stuart, is a contemporary sculptor of wide renown. Though Aisling downplays her own artistic talent, a hauntingly beautiful painting of Emilia graces a corner of the library. She pursues the cause of art by holding weeklong workshops each spring and summer at Rossnaree.

On our final morning at Rossnaree, we saw Aisling rushing about in jeans, holding flowers and greens freshly cut from the garden. "What's the occasion?" I asked. "A group of thirty women from the Irish Countrywomen's Association are coming at

11:00 for tea and a tour of the house and grounds," she replied somewhat anxiously. "Can we help?" I asked. She thought a moment. "No, I think I'll be OK. But why not stay for the tour? Though you may just hear what you already know." "We'd love to," Lori eagerly accepted.

When the large van pulled in at 10:45, Aisling fretted, "I hate it when people show up early!" However, she was relieved when she saw there were only seventeen ladies, instead of the thirty expected. Lori and I went outside to join the lecture that had started while Aisling put on the finishing touches in the house.

The ladies were gathered on the edge of the lawn in rapt attention, as John McCallen, a local historian, spun colorful stories from the area's past. In contrast, Rocky and Dagda lay sprawled out amongst them taking a snooze, as much as to say "We've heard all that many times before."

John continued a detailed account of how the ford at Rossnaree impacted the Battle of the Boyne. Lori and I exchanged knowing glances, reflecting back on our visit the day before to the Battle of the Boyne Visitor Center. Located at the main battleground on a bend of the river by Oldbridge, four miles downstream from Rossnaree, the Center was just newly opened the previous year. Like Newgrange and other recently developed attractions, this center was creatively designed. Several walks followed the routes of opposing forces in the battle. Inside the Center, which occupies the eighteenth century Oldbridge House, multimedia displays bring the scenes to life.

Rossnaree is prominently featured, as well it should be. A tactical error by King James jeopardized his chances in the battle. Thinking the Boyne was impassable upstream, he had the bridge at Slane destroyed, so William's troops would be channeled into one area. When William discovered that the Boyne, indeed, could be crossed at Rossnaree, a multi-pronged attack was executed and the Jacobite forces were overwhelmed. A relief map on a broad table outlines the battle with lights that glow at strategic points while the audio and the three flat screens above describe each stage of the unfolding skirmish.

Aisling emerged from the house, graciously welcoming the group, stylish tan blouse and dark skirt having replaced her well-worn work clothes. She noted that when the Boyne center opened, she had invited all the guides for tea, also, so that they could better visualize Rossnaree when enlightening visitors.

Aisling shared stories of the estate grounds, like a recent wedding under the yew tree arch, where in earlier decades tennis matches were held. Then she led everyone into the house, bringing to life paintings and antique furniture as they moved from room to room.

After tea and cakes in the dining room, we bid goodbye to the ladies, realizing that our stay at Rossnaree was also at an end. Leaving was difficult, since Aisling's warm hospitality had made us feel like long lost members of the family. We stood in awe of this remarkable woman with a renowned heritage of her own, running the historic manor by herself.

Ashford Castle

Dromoland Castle Entryway at Halloween

Chapter 5
The Halloween of Irish Legend

The ancient Celtic Samhain festival lives on in modern form

With afternoon shadows deepening on that final October day in 1950's Illinois, I would run the half-mile home from school, don an old mask or cowboy hat, grab a paper shopping bag, and as darkness fell, eagerly race door to door screaming "trick or treat" at the top of my lungs. A successful Halloween those days simply meant a bulging sack of candy by the end of the evening.

Like most holidays in America, Halloween has increasingly been infused by media driven commercialism. Modern day partakers are often hard pressed to explain the source of the holiday. A recent visit to Ireland, where Halloween began, revealed to my wife, Lori and I that the Irish have promoted their ancient tradition even more, while still retaining some of the early mystique.

Judging from internet ads I saw while planning our October trip, celebrations in Dublin could rival those of Mardi Gras in New Orleans. Perhaps I shouldn't have been surprised: Dublin is, after all, the city that Dracula's creator, Bram Stoker, called home. Planned ghost tours, parades and fireworks would be touting Dublin's haunted past, while the pubs and streets in Temple Bar would sport fun costumes and raucous merriment.

Lori and I decided to delve deeper into the mysteries of Halloween beyond the lively frivolities of the city. Wanting to stay at some ancient castles, we were surprised to find special multi-night packages spanning the entire week of Halloween, complete with festivities and themed games for the whole family.

Venerable Ashford Castle in County Mayo promoted its "Hogwarts Halloween" Special, with activities ranging from a treasure hunt in the "Forbidden Forest" to a "Chamber of Witchcraft & Wizardry." Wisely, castle staff promised to entertain the little "goblins" with a Harry Potter movie in the evening while Mom and Dad relaxed to a gourmet dinner in the elegant George V dining room. No newcomer to historic lore, the castle dates back to 1228, and was once owned by the Guinness family.

However, the origins of Halloween lie hundreds of years earlier than even Ashford Castle. A Celtic festival known as Samhain celebrated the harvest and the change of seasons at the end of October. Originating in pre-Christian times, the druid tradition also included ghosts, fairies and demons that surfaced as days became darker. Christian missionaries tried to replace pagan rites, establishing All Saints Day on November 1. The sacred or "hallowed" day gave rise to the modern name for the night before: "All Hallow's Eve," or Halloween for short.

We could only imagine what the ancient ones at five-thousand-year-old Newgrange in County Meath, north of Dublin, would have thought of the strange goings on at the site's visitor center, when we arrived for a visit. Normally a well ordered entry point for tours to the passage tombs, the halls were a hubbub of ladies in pointy black hats, known as "Crafty Witches," scurrying around tables of eager kids, midst creations of Halloween decorations, masks and pumpkins.

Our search for the origins of Halloween had brought us to the right place. A colorful brochure proclaimed the "Spirits of Meath Halloween Festival – Where Halloween Began." The Crafty Witches at Newgrange were just one of numerous venues and events celebrating this uniquely Irish experience. Among the many choices, Causey and Grove Farms in Fordstown offered broom riding, magic potion mixing, spell casting, and a tunnel of terror. Festive Trim displayed dancing to drive away evil spirits and bring good fortune near the town's carefully restored castle, famous for its role in the movie Braveheart. Various pubs and cafes throughout the area hosted fancy costume competitions, pumpkin carving and other spooky treats.

County Meath's status as the origin of Halloween stems from the claim that the Samhain ceremony began over 2,000 years ago on the Hill of Ward in Athboy. To symbolize the end of the old year, all fires in the country were extinguished. Druids lit a new fire on the Hill of Ward first, signaling the beginning of the New Year. The hill was known as a "thin place" where the separation between the physical world and the spiritual Otherworld was lifted, allowing spirits to move back and forth.

Though living long before the Celts, the prehistoric peoples of Newgrange shared a common regard for the mysteries of the changing seasons. The passage tomb's massive structure, equivalent to the pyramids of Egypt, though 500 years older, has an entryway perfectly aligned to catch the rays of the sun precisely on the morning of the winter solstice.

Needing time to absorb the plethora of Halloween related spectacle, we retreated to our bed and breakfast lodging at Rossnaree. Just a couple miles away, the historic house crowns a secluded knoll looking out over the Boyne River, past broad meadows to majestic Newgrange in the distance.

Though Rossnaree is best known for its role as a key location in the seventeenth century Battle of the Boyne, our owner host, Aishling Law, pointed out a local artifact possibly related to the early mythology. "The wall of the old mill at Rossnaree contained a sheela-na-gig," she informed us. Mysterious stone carvings replicating naked women, sheela-na-gigs are thought by some to be Celtic fertility goddesses, or ones that ward off evil spirits. Alas, this sheela-na-gig had been taken from the wall and secreted away to prevent its theft. Even so, another sheela-na-gig would turn up at our next stop.

The next day we continued our pursuit of ancient Halloween-related Irish mysteries. We drove to remote Boa Island in County Fermanagh, where Caldragh Graveyard is located. The small eighteenth century Christian graveyard is distinguished by the eerie presence of a pagan carved stone about three feet high. Nearby stood a smaller stone, the sheela-na-gig known as the Lusty Man, which had been brought here later. But the main attraction was the larger "Janus" Stone, as it is known, named after a Roman god, since it has faces on both sides.

As we gingerly stepped past aged tombstones heading toward the Janus Stone, I was glad we were not attempting this feat after dark. Aside from fearing the dank creepiness of a nocturnal graveyard, chances of an ankle sprain loomed from the multitude of half hidden, grass covered grave stone fragments. The mystery hidden in the stony faces of the Janus Stone was heightened by a cleft on top of the head. Shiny coins glistened from within. Superstitious folk were perhaps paying homage by leaving the coins, hoping for good fortune.

Often in conversations with the Irish, their connection to old superstitions was evident. At dinner one night, I commented to a couple from Belfast that there was a new moon tonight. They warned us, tongue in cheek, "Never look at the new moon through glass. It's bad luck."

We were ready to leave the graveyard when Lori spotted a whitethorn tree. A closer look revealed several ribbons and trinkets attached to branches. "It's a fairy tree," she exclaimed. "People have left them gifts." Caldragh Graveyard is thought to be a "thin place." In ages gone by, it was believed that on Halloween, dead souls could pass through the thin place. Families would set out fruits and nuts as "treats" for them. Evil spirits could also pass through. So masks were worn to ward them off. Also, carved turnips lighted with candles were carried or set out to dispel the bad spirits. Today Halloween masks, trick or treating and carved pumpkins are remnants of these ancient practices.

After a restful night at the nearby Manor House, a striking 19th century country hotel set on the shores of Lower Lough Erne, we headed southward toward County Clare.

Our final stop on the night of Halloween was the storied Dromoland Castle. We approached in the midst of a dreary rainstorm. Entering the long, winding drive, we viewed with some trepidation the foreboding gray visage as the fortified castle rose up before us. Those feelings were quickly dispelled by the bellman, greeting us with an umbrella and welcoming smile. Once inside, the warmth and elegance surrounded us with reassurance, as did the carved pumpkin in the lobby. Nearby, we saw a group of children being guided in a Halloween game around the castle.

On check in we were informed that the traditional bonfire had been held the night before. Knowing that in past times, this ritual was another means of scaring off the demons, we took heart hoping that they would not be back to visit us on this night.

We settled in for a dinner fit for royalty in the Earl of Thomand room. At first, costumed kids came in with their parents, but before long left to watch a scary movie in a specially designated lair. Then at last we were able to share the regally adorned dining room with the other adults, all enjoying a peaceful meal commemorating the finale of a memorable Halloween.

Walking the murky castle halls back to our room later felt a little spooky. Antiquated paintings of ancestors stared down on us with stern expressions. We approached each corner carefully. Earlier at Ashford Castle, we had been momentarily startled by an unexpected "skeleton" sprawled across a staircase. Once at our room in a distant wing, we took extra care to bolt the locks on both door and windows. Though sleep took longer to come in the unfamiliar darkness, we slept soundly that night, with not so much as a restless ghost to disturb us. Nonetheless, we knew that Halloween would never be quite the same for us back home.

Godafoss, Iceland

St. Kevin's church, Glendalough, Ireland

Chapter 6
Iceland, Land of Fire and Ice…and Celtic DNA?

Vikings extend Irish roots to Iceland

Note: A version of this chapter was first published in Celtic Life International, February 2020.

The Nordic Vikings come to mind when the origins of the Icelandic people are considered. The remote northerly location led to Iceland's Viking discovery much later than the British Isles, which were raided and plundered by the adventurous Scandinavians as early as 793 AD at Lindisfarne on the north coast of England and 795 AD at the Isle of Iona off Scotland's coast.

The first Viking settlement in Iceland was considered to be in 874 AD at the location of the current capital, Reykjavik. By contrast, the Viking settlement of Dublin, which became the Republic of Ireland's capital, dates to 841 AD. Curiously, DNA analysis reveals that Icelandic women are almost two-thirds Celtic in heritage. The men, though less so, still are about 20% Celtic according to their DNA.

Those earlier conquests of Ireland and Scotland may hold the answer. Having settled the Celtic lands and founding cities, the Vikings ventured out again. This time the theory is that Irish women were taken as slaves, helping to populate the virgin land of fire and ice. Some male Celts may have been taken as well. Other theories, though sketchier, surmise that a few

Irish monks may have landed in Iceland earlier, in their quest to spread the Christian gospel.

Beyond sharing Celtic DNA, Iceland and Ireland, as well as other Celtic countries, offer a variety of parallels and contrasts. The two island countries are relatively similar in size and shape, with Iceland weighing in as the larger at 40 thousand square miles compared to Ireland's 32 thousand. They both are subject to moist, changeable weather that is tempered by the impact of the North Atlantic Current extension of the Gulf Stream, and the south-westerly winds. Still, lying some 900 miles to the northwest, Iceland exhibits a clearly colder climate.

My wife, Lori, and I celebrated a geographical indicator of Iceland's subarctic climate midway through a cruise circling Iceland this past year. Landing on tiny Grimsey Island at the far north, passengers were anxious to hike over to a small signed bridge that demarcated the location of the Arctic Circle. Certificates presented by the ship's staff commemorated the event.

All of two square miles, Grimsey has about 60 residents but thousands of birds including Arctic Terns, and Puffins in the summer. After a short, cold and windy walk along the barren, yet dramatic cliffs, we were content to settle for a hot cup of tea and a traditional specialty, Icelandic waffles covered with chocolate syrup, rhubarb jam and whipped cream.

I asked our friendly host at the Gullsól Guesthouse, one of two on the island, how business was. She tactfully replied "We love it when the ships come in." Considering that on the two prior cruises our ship was unable to land on account of high waves, I could imagine how big a factor the unpredictable weather played on visitor traffic.

With our ship pulling away from Grimsey, I spotted a coastal feature that conjured up an old Irish legend. Spanning the front of a sheer cliff, orderly basaltic columns rose from the water in a neat row. Visions from earlier sojourns recalled the Giant's Causeway on the tip of Northern Ireland, and the corresponding Isle of Staffa, off the Scottish Coast. Separated by a mere 82 miles of the North Channel, these two volcanic formations of hexagonal columns form the endpoints for the legend of Irish Finn McCool and the Scottish giant, Benandonnar. Folk lore has it that McCool built the causeway between the two points to dare Benandonnar to cross over for a fight. Seeing the larger size of Benandonnar, McCool fled, as he was chased back over the causeway. McCool's wife covered him in bed, telling the arriving Benandonnar that McCool was her baby. Fearing that the father of such a large baby must be huge, Benandonnar retreated tearing up the causeway as he went. All that is left are the two separated extremities.

While Irish folklore is rich with such stories and also fantasy fairy creatures, like leprechauns, Iceland upholds its own mythical traditions centered on the 'hidden people,' known as elves, and trolls. In fact, of the several basaltic formations found in volcanic Iceland, one gives rise to a troll legend of its own. Near Vik on the southern coast of Iceland, three basaltic columns, known as stacks, stand dramatically just off the shore of the black sand beach, Reynisfjara. The columns are said to have been trolls trying to lure a ship aground one night. But before they could finish the job, the morning sun rose, turning them to stone for all eternity.

A more modern, scientific approach ties the origins of the hexagonal pillars of Iceland and Ireland together. A recent study by a group of volcanologists from the University of Liverpool ascertained that the columns were formed after the molten lava had solidified but was still hot. Using a sample basaltic column from the Eyjafjallajökull volcano in southern Iceland, the scientists determined that the lava fractured into the geometric pattern at between 840 and 890°C. Eyjafjallajökull is the volcano that erupted in 2010, disrupting air travel for several days.

A modern architectural expression of the symmetric columns rises up as the defining landmark on Reykjavik's skyline. Hallgrímskirkja, a Lutheran parish church, towers at 240 feet as the tallest building in the capital city. A statue of the most famous Icelander, explorer Leif Erickson, stands in front of the church, a gift from the United States to commemorate the 1000th anniversary of Iceland's parliament, which as the world's oldest, convened in 930 AD.

The parliament met at another site of natural and volcanic beauty, Thingvellir, about 25 miles northeast of Reykjavik. Meaning assembly plains, Thingvellir was an outdoor setting for the meetings, situated on the crest of the Mid-Atlantic Ridge zone that spanned the geologic meeting place of the Eurasian and North American tectonic plates. Set beside a broad plain, a volcanic fissure formed a natural amphitheater and ravine, ideal for corralling the attendee's horses, and for speeches from a rocky outcrop, the Lögberg, or Law Rock. Nearby Thingvallavatn, the largest lake in

Iceland, provided ample fish for the assemblage. Walking through the narrow fissure today gives an eerie feeling of the momentous energy that flowed through the area long ago.

Thingvellir shares the title of oldest parliament in the world with the Celtic Isle of Man's Tynwald, whose name shares the same root and meaning. While the Icelandic assembly met at Thingvellir until 1798, before its relocation at Reykjavik in 1844, the Manx people claim the title of the oldest continuously meeting parliament for the High Court of Tynwald which still meets in Douglas, capital of the Isle of Man.

Fans of Game of Thrones, the fantasy epic television series, may recognize Reynisfjara above, and Thingvellir, as two of numerous filming locations in Iceland. The wild and remote beauty of the Icelandic landscape harmonized well with the dramatic grandeur of the Game of Thrones storyline. Northern Ireland also offered settings for the ancient tale. On a prior trip, Lori and I almost inadvertently wandered onto a set while roaming in the area of the Giant's Causeway. Later that day, while sipping tea at award winning host, Bob Isles' nearby Whitepark House, another couple told of accidently driving onto the natural set before being hurriedly escorted away.

The leprechauns of Ireland and the elves of Iceland are thought to have similar origins far back in fairy lore. They share some characteristics, such as being invisible to humans. The Icelandic elf legend goes back to the beginning of humankind. When God visited Adam and Eve, Eve hid some of her children from God's sight since she hadn't finished washing them. Consequently, God decided that these children should remain invisible to humans. Hence, they became known as the "hidden people," or elves.

A modern day haven for Icelandic elves is Hafnarfjörður, the harbor and suburb just south of Reykjavik, from whence our ship embarked and returned. Known as the "Town in the Lava," Hafnarfjörður sits on an ancient lava field. Its unusual volcanic formations supply ideal habitats for elves, who are said to prefer rocky terrain for their dwelling places. Known to be mischievous, elves, even in modern times, have been blamed for broken machinery on construction sites that were considered to be elfin domains.

Another aspect of folklore draws a parallel between two scenic lakes, one more famous than the other. Most of us are familiar with the Loch Ness Monster, purported to ply the depths of the long, deep lake in the Scottish Highlands. But I had never heard of the Lagarfljótsormur. That is, not until passing by the long, narrow lake Lagarfljót, on a trip out from the port of Seydisfjordur, our ship's stop on the east coast of Iceland. While tales of "Nessie" go all the way back to St. Columba in the sixth century, the "Lagarfljót Worm," as this ominous sea creature is known, is relatively recent, having a first mention in the mid-fourteenth century. The monster is large like Nessie and serpentine, but with humps. Legends claim that both terrorize and kill those unfortunate enough to encounter them on their respective lakes. Reports of sightings continue even into recent times.

While Iceland, Ireland and Scotland all have volcanic origins, Iceland's location directly on the colliding boundaries of two rift zones gives rise to the more recent active volcanos and other features, such as the geyser basin just east of Reykjavik. Lakes, such as those mentioned above, relate to another common heritage: glacial action.

Iceland, from its northerly locale, is still home to active glaciers. Sadly, the start of our circumnavigation of the island coincided with a memorial tribute to the first death of an Icelandic glacier. The plaque commemorating the momentous event included a Letter to the future: "*Ok is the first Icelandic glacier to lose its status as a glacier. In the next 200 years all our glaciers are expected to follow the same path. The monument is to acknowledge that we know what is happening and what needs to be done. Only you know if we did it.*"

Though Ireland's glaciers are long gone, another beautiful remnant from an earlier Ice Age is the valley of Glendalough, in County Wicklow, south of Dublin. After cruising around Iceland, our journey took us to Ireland where we drove through this hauntingly picturesque setting. With a Gaelic name meaning "valley of two lakes," Glendalough is known for the well preserved ruins of a monastic settlement established by St. Kevin in the sixth century.

As we walked among the vestiges of the ancient village, the solid granite structures, such as the hundred-foot-high Round Tower and St. Kevin's Church with its circular belfry, gave testament to the resolve of the monastery community over many centuries. Rising up after destructive Viking raids, Glendalough continued as a beacon of faith until the dissolution of the monasteries by Henry VIII in the sixteenth century. In modern times, Glendalough is a titular diocese of the Roman Catholic Church. Diarmuid Martin, Archbishop of Dublin served as Titular Bishop of Glendalough in the early days of the twenty-first century.

Leaving the valley of Glendalough, a pleasant drive winds through the scenic Wicklow Mountains and up over the pass of Sally Gap. Even driving slowly to absorb the natural essence, we almost missed one of Ireland's finest waterfalls, Glenmacnass. Cascading 250 feet down the glaciated slopes of the lush valley, the water displayed a yellowish hue from boggish sediment carried along on the rainy afternoon. Nearby, Ireland's highest waterfall at 400 feet, Powerscourt Waterfall flows over the Wicklow Mountain foothills in a horsetail fan.

Waterfalls are gems of Iceland as well. Gullfoss, in southwest Iceland, exhibits a uniquely intricate pattern as it first flows in curving cascades with water from the Langjökull glacier, then falls dramatically for a hundred feet over a narrow crevice of the Hvítá River canyon.

Our favorite was Goðafoss, just east of Akureyri in the north of Iceland. "It looks like Niagara Falls," Lori exclaimed, comparing it to the iconic waterfall in North America. Though only falling a quarter the distance that Niagara drops, Goðafoss, meaning "waterfall of the gods" in Icelandic, bears a striking resemblance to its more famous counterpart.

As islands, Iceland and Ireland have ample displays of dramatic sea cliffs. Ireland's most celebrated are the Cliffs of Moher, on the western coastline. With over a million and a half annual visitors, the Cliffs are second only to the Guinness

Storehouse in Dublin in popularity. My favorite is the more remote Slieve League, further north in County Donegal. At a height of almost 2,000 feet, Slieve League is three times as high as the Cliffs of Moher. Breathtaking as is the view from the top, when I first drove the final quarter mile to get there, before the route was paved, the one lane gravel track dropped off steeply on both sides for a truly heart-stopping experience. Thankfully the road was widened when paved, though I would still hate to have to maneuver around an oncoming vehicle on the narrowest stretch.

Iceland's cliffs stand out in the form of fjords. Having delighted in the splendor radiated by the fjords of Norway, New Zealand and Alaska on previous adventures, I found the Icelandic version to conjure up memories of the others, such as the sparse population of Alaska's Inside Passage, the quaint villages of Geiranger Fjord in Norway, and the remoteness of New Zealand's Milford Sound.

As for population, the whole of Iceland has only 360,000 residents, of which two-thirds are in the Reykjavik metropolitan area. The total is less than 10% of the citizenry of Ireland or Norway. The scant Icelandic population has enabled the preservation of most of the pristine natural characteristics of the countryside. While Ireland has 57 cities exceeding 10,000 inhabitants, Iceland has but five.

One realm where both Iceland and Ireland have sacrificed native conservation is reflected in the lack of trees covering the landscape. Where once woodlands flourished, covering possibly as much as 40% of the land, Iceland now has but 2% forestation while Ireland's is little more than 10%. The paucity of trees in Ireland often goes unnoticed, overshadowed by the "Forty Shades of Green," as the Johnny Cash song so richly describes the color that is almost synonymous with the Emerald Isle's verdant scenery.

In the early days of settlement, lumber was in vast demand for construction of homes and buildings, grazing land for livestock, and for production of charcoal for heating. In the modern day world, similar issues have emerged, raising global concerns from the implications of these activities in the Amazon region of South America.

Iceland's harsh climate, volcanic activity, and resulting erosion make reforestation efforts more difficult than in Ireland. Nevertheless, an ambitious program is underway that has seen several million trees planted annually in the past couple of years alone. A hike near Egilsstaðir in East Iceland took us through Hallormsstaðaskógur, Iceland's largest national forest at 286 square miles, and one of over fifty such projects across the country. Began in 1905 to preserve native birch trees, this forest now boasts a diversity of over 85 different types of trees. Along the path we encountered an unusual sculpture of three slender tree trunks carved into totem-like poles, with curved designs and faces as if in tribute to the sacredness of the forest.

The reforestation effort was also evident to us when in port at Akureyri. On the dock by our ship we saw a sign asking for donations for a tree planting campaign. Lori and I now own a tree in Iceland, having made the requested $2 Euro contribution.

As our cruise around Iceland, followed by a drive across Ireland, drew to a close, we took away new insights from these enchanting islands and their people. With such extensive shared DNA, the least that can be said is that Icelanders are literally Celtic at heart. But as this brief sojourn has shown, the natural and cultural parallels reflect a closer kinship between these hauntingly mystical and mesmerizing lands.

Barry's boat at the dock

White Island stone figures

Chapter 7

Choppy Waters Stir Up a Lough's Bloody Remnants

Plying the past on Northern Ireland's Lower Lough Erne

Standing beneath the eaves of the Manor House Country Hotel Marina in the steady morning rain, my wife, Lori, and I wondered if our wait had been in vain. Several months back, we arranged online for a private journey by motor craft across Northern Ireland's Lower Lough Erne. Now as we gazed forlornly out across the frothy waters of the lough on this final day of August, I questioned aloud, "Will anyone even show up in this nasty looking weather?" Lori just kept looking over the broad expanse.

Lough Erne Water Taxi had offered a three-hour survey of the lough's ancient sites that spread along the meandering shores and islands of the 70-mile-long waterway. We had driven the scenic shores before and accessed sacred sights on a couple of the islands by bridge and ferry, but one had eluded us. Even so, a key focus this day was to get a better sense for how warring forces, for good or evil, employed these waterways to accomplish their missions, righteous or nefarious. Over the millennia, both color the rich history of Lower Loch Erne

Like clockwork as the appointed 10:00 AM hour approached, we spotted a tiny blip far off amid the choppy waves of the sea-like channel. Within minutes the blip grew to a recognizable vessel speeding our way. Right on schedule, the ten-passenger boat pulled up at our dock and a smiling Barry Flanagan hopped off, greeting us.

"Don't let the rain bother you. We'll get around just fine. There's only one spot that will be out of reach. The high waves make the dock at White Island impossible to negotiate."

Lori and I looked at each other with pained expressions, but tried to keep Barry from noticing. "That will be fine," I remarked. "We're ready to go." White Island was the one we had missed on previous visits, so it had been a priority on this trip. Even so, we weren't about to question the boat captain about avoiding what sounded like a dangerous landing attempt.

Lough Erne's dark past is a mix of legend and reality. One myth has the lough named after a goddess, Érann, or even Ériu (Éire), who gave early Ireland its name. Folklore describes the origin of the lough arising from the tragic death of Queen Maebh's lady in waiting, Erne. Fleeing a giant that emerged from the Oweynagatn cave, Erne drowned, with her body dissolving to form Lough Erne.

Boa Island, famous for the enigmatic pagan Janus Stone perched in a Christian graveyard, has an even more sinister name, *Badhbh*. A war goddess, Badhbh took the form of a crow, wreaking confusion and carnage while flying over a battlefield to gain her desired result.

Donning life preservers and taking seats in the enclosed section of the boat, we were ready for an adventure. Barry maneuvered slowly out from the dock and then revved up the motor to speed toward our first destination, Tully Castle. A repetitive loud "bang" accompanied the ride as the boat plowed through wave after wave in the turgid surf. Amazed that we didn't get seasick, Lori and I peered out the windows, enjoying the vigorous motion amid the brisk autumn air.

In no time, we were closing in on Tully Castle the way earlier residents and marauders did, by water. Back then, the land was covered with thick forests, making travel by the clear waterways much quicker and easier. Nowadays there is also road access from the shore, which is the modern approach.

Stepping off on the dock, Barry led us up the short, wooded path to the castle ruins. At first glance, the jagged gray walls, reaching up in places to second floor level and higher, must have looked pretty much the same as they did after that fateful day in 1641 when the castle's life, as well as many of her residents' lives, came to an end. The ruins have been sitting here empty since then, spruced up only by restoration during recent decades.

The short, tragic life of Tully Castle began in 1613. Sir John Hume, an Englishman, built the castle, having been granted the land during the Plantation period, after the English defeated the Irish at the beginning of the seventeenth century. Previously, the whole of County Fermanagh had belonged to the Maguire clan for several hundred years.

By 1641, the Irish rebelled, seeking to take back their land. Rory Maguire took aim at Tully Castle. On Christmas Eve, he and his men came ashore, attacking the castle, which fell easily, since most of the men were gone. Promising to spare the occupants lives, they led Lady Hume and her family out of the castle to a nearby location. However, on Christmas day, Maguire returned and massacred all those remaining in the castle, while setting it on fire.

Maguire was part of the Irish Confederacy that temporarily took back control of some areas. Maguire met his own demise in 1648, the year before Oliver Cromwell's troops invaded, ultimately putting down the uprising.

In modern times, the only conflict disturbing the peaceful setting of Tully Castle involves the grounds within the bawn remains (defensive walls). The attractive ornamental garden and hedges constructed to enhance the historic site have been uprooted and replaced with grassy turf, an apparently more authentic look.

Retracing our steps along the pathway to the boat, raindrops began to fall. Like a favorable omen, the shower had abated during the castle visit. To our pleasant surprise, this phenomenon continued throughout our trip, providing the good fortune of keeping us dry for most stops along the way.

Soon our boat was speeding on an easterly course across the wide watery expanse to the next stop, Castle Archdale. Here our perspective moved several centuries forward. Though the castle was also built by a Plantation owner and succumbed to a similar fate from attack by Rory Maguire as did Tully Castle, the property's claim to fame is more recent.

The surrounding confines now form a country and caravan park with a marina, but served a more secretive and deadly role during World War II. From this dock, we walked across a wide expanse of concrete to modern buildings constructed for war service. As part of the United Kingdom, Northern Ireland was an allied country, and supportive of the war effort. The nearby Republic of Ireland remained neutral during the war.

The Americans, in a joint effort with the British to protect the Atlantic sea lanes during the Battle of the Atlantic, saw a strategic role for the broad waters of Lower Lough Erne. German U-boats were successfully attacking allied ships, especially in an area known as the Black Gap, which lay beyond the range of land-based aircraft. The location of the lough was closer to the Atlantic, which could make the difference for allied defensive forces to reach the treacherous U-boats.

The Royal Air Force (RAF) built a base on the shore at Castle Archdale. The Americans shipped over a fleet of "flying boats," using the expansive lough for takeoffs and landings. However, one obstacle remained. Between Northern Ireland's Lough Erne and the Atlantic Ocean was a strip of Republic of Ireland territory. In a super-secret enclave, the neutral Republic was convinced to grant permission for flights over its airspace, unbeknownst to the enemy.

The key seven mile stretch of County Donegal separating the allies from the Atlantic became known as the Donegal Corridor. The ensuing flights to the Black Gap served to substantially reduce allied casualties in the area. The most notable mission was when a "Catalina" seaplane with an American crewman was credited with spotting the notorious German Battleship, Bismarck, which subsequently led to its sinking.

A museum housed in one of the World War II buildings, told the story. I could feel my chest swelling out a little further than usual as I viewed the exhibits and read with pride the role my American ancestors played with their British comrades in this crucial, but little told episode. I have always harbored a special place in my heart for my uniformed countrymen, since learning that my parents named me after an American soldier, a family friend, who gave his life in battle during WWII.

"Good news," Barry exclaimed, guiding us back to the boat. "The waves have calmed. I think we can land at White Island after all." We were thrilled, having long since given up on the prospect. Just a short ride along the lough's northeastern sector across Castle Archdale Bay brought us to the small island.

As we approached the landing, my perception adjusted once again, this time to many centuries earlier. Christian monks had arrived here as well as to Devenish Island, our next destination, founding monasteries around the sixth century. They made inroads for several centuries until the Vikings discovered the richness of the land, invading and destroying. The *Annals of Ulster*, written on nearby Belle Island, describes one such invasion in 837 that may have finished off the island monasteries.

There is little left of the monastery on White Island. The minimal ruins of a 13th century church contain what may be remnants. Built into the wall are seven carved statues that represent the sole unique feature that set the site apart. The statues are thought to be components of the original monastery that were subsequently left in the rubble after Viking attacks, until retrieved centuries later.

Stepping through the archway within the stone walls, we peered at the figures while Barry did his best to describe what each depicted. They were carved in a style similar to pre-Christian images. In fact, one appears to be a Sheela-na-gig, fertility goddess, similar to the two-thousand-year-old Janus Stone on nearby Boa Island. The others are thought to portray St. Patrick, the biblical David, and Jesus.

More ruins and historical facts were available for Devenish Island, at the far south end of the Lough, where we headed for the final stop. Even from a distance, the island's landmark round tower stood out marking the spot. Though a more recent addition, only dating from the 12th century, the 80-foot-high stone tower offered a striking visage. All of the visible ruins, including several church structures and a high cross are from this era. Earlier formations are evident in the earthworks, including a prior tower.

Saint Molaise is known to have founded the monastery on Devenish Island in the mid-sixth century. Known as one of the "12 apostles of Ireland," his reputation spread, and the monastery flourished for many centuries. Molaise was known to have counseled St. Columba to leave Ireland after Columba caused a battle where several thousand soldiers were killed, the result of a dispute over Columba's copying a manuscript without permission. Columba exiled himself to the Scottish island of Iona, building a successful ministry there.

The Viking raids came about three hundred years after Saint Molaise's death. The Vikings were merciless, slaughtering and plundering all in their sight. Nevertheless, the monastery was rebuilt and even survived burnings several centuries later. The Maquires of Tully Castle notoriety continued to hold family burials at Devenish into the nineteenth century.

With our tour coming to an end, Barry turned the boat back toward the Manor House Country Hotel near Killadeas. On the way, he pointed out from a distance the sumptuous Lough Erne Resort on the western shore, where several years earlier the venerable Group of Eight (G8) country leaders met, seeking mutual peaceful goals. Once back at the Manor House, we bid a gracious farewell to our well versed guide and captain. From the marina, we walked up to the Manor House Dining Room for lunch, where we could look out over the majestic lough, contemplating the rich, colored history that it held.

Lori noticed with curiosity an American flag flying from the hotel roof. She wondered why it was there. As it turns out, the Manor House, itself, has a part in the region's history. Captain John Irvine acquired the estate where the hotel now stands in 1660, not that long after the rebellion of 1641. The mansion has been rebuilt several times over the centuries. According to the Hotel website, during World War II, the Government requisitioned the mansion for use by the American forces, and operated the headquarters there for the seaplane base described earlier in this article.

After lunch, Lori and I made a pilgrimage to Boa Island, completing the day's sojourn in Irish history. A number of years ago, Lori's novel, *The Thin Place*, was set at Caldragh Graveyard on the island, with the Janus Stone playing a key role. Each time we return to Ireland, we visit the Graveyard again. The cleft at the top of the Janus Stone was still filled with rainwater, and coins left for good luck. The Whitethorn tree still thrived nearby, as the legendary "thin place" where the fairy creatures could pass between our world and the "other" world.

With our departure, we placed a coin on the Janus Stone by the others, to commemorate the many lives lost in conflicts over the centuries on this history-rich lough, and to express gratitude for the peace that reins today and hopefully for centuries to come.

Part 2 - Scotland

Rosslyn Chapel

Giant's Causeway

Chapter 8

The Spirit-filled Isle of Iona

From spectacle to solitude in a Celtic land

"I hope James Bond never goes to Iona," I grumbled to my wife, Lori, as we left the theatre. We had just screened the latest installment of the iconic British agent's exploits. Bond's return home to the picturesque valley of Glencoe rekindled in us our own recent sojourn through those verdant Scottish Highlands. Walking to the car, I found myself clutching a small, smooth stone that I carried in my pocket.

We had experienced first hand how wide exposure through the media can transform an enchanting gem into a chaotic tourist center. Leaving Edinburgh, we paused at Rosslyn Chapel, a relatively obscure site until The Da Vinci Code brought the world's attention. Built in gothic style for a noble family in 1446, the ornate little stone church abounded with mysterious, symbolic carvings. Some were associated with the legend of the Knights Templar, featured by Dan Brown in his blockbuster novel. A haven for prayer and reflection, the once quiet chapel now played host to many hundreds of visitors daily. The staff still faithfully delivered religious services, but the solitude the chapel was designed to provide had been lost.

We were anxious to push on toward the isle of Iona, off Scotland's west coast. Iona is not a place that is visited as an afterthought. Having traveled the width of Scotland from Edinburgh, we drove our rental car aboard the ferry in Oban, northwest of Glasgow. A forty five minute crossing brought us to the Isle of Mull, where the dominant view of Duart Castle, ancient home of the McLean clan, held forth on a promontory above the village of Craignure.

From here a single lane road zigzagged forty miles to Fionphort. Though furry Highland cattle roamed the island freely, the more frightening danger was the occasional tour bus speeding around a blind curve on the narrow lane. At Fionphort, our rental car had to be left behind before we boarded a small ferry for the final ten minute passage.

As Iona approached, the historic graystone Abbey Church stood out prominently to the North, set off against the island's low green hills. Beneath darkening skies, the ferry landed at the tiny village center. A cold breeze blew raindrops in our faces. We were glad that the quaint Argyll Hotel, one of several two-story stone cottages along the waterfront, was only a hundred yards away.

A woman offered to carry a suitcase for Lori. Of the hundred or so residents on the island, the woman typified their warm sense of community. When Lori said "You probably don't get much sunshine here," she replied, "Oh, the sun is always shining on Iona. When clouds are in the way, we don't see it, but the sun is always there."

We started to feel the peaceful allure of this isolated speck of land. Amidst the stark environs of the Inner Hebrides, we discovered Iona to be a focal point of ancient mythology, Celtic faith, music, literature, and contemporary pilgrimages.

We first become aware of Iona on an earlier trip to Ireland, where we explored remote Glencolmcille in Donegal. In the sixth century, Columba, one of Ireland's patron saints, ministered there. On our visit, we trekked through the village and across the rugged hills following the "Turas Cholmcille," St. Columba's fifteen station pilgrimage which included ancient standing stones, a holy well, chapel, stone bed and wishing stone.

At station 9, *Cloch na Aonaigh, "The Stone of the Gathering,"* a six foot high carved slab with a hole near the top, Lori gingerly followed tradition: "The pilgrim circles the cairn three times, praying, and then, placing his back to the stone, makes a declaration renouncing the World, the Flesh, and the Devil." Not missing a trick, she then peered through the hole hoping to "see heaven." Lastly, she called impishly to me, while putting her finger through the opening. Touching my finger to hers, we felt like the young lovers of old, sealing their engagement through the stone.

Around 560, a dispute Columba had with his former teacher led to a battle where thousands were killed. Exiled to Scotland, Columba landed on Iona in 563 and founded the monastery.

After settling into one of the Argyll Hotel's 16 small but clean rooms, we were ready for afternoon tea. A glassed in atrium at the front of the hotel made for a cozy setting, even with the rain swept sea in full view before us. Imparting a family run atmosphere, the Argyll Hotel prided itself on coexisting responsibly along side the natural environment. Consistent with that goal, produce for meals was drawn from the

Hotel's organic garden, while meats and seafood were locally sourced from sustainability conscious providers.

That evening at the hotel, we enjoyed a dinner of Cullen skink (a thick Scottish soup of smoked haddock, potatoes and onions), slow cooked confit of chicken leg , and peach melba, all while exchanging pleasantries with two ladies at the next table. From England's Lake District, they made an annual pilgrimage to Iona. "We keep returning for the nightly services at the Abbey."

Founded by St. Columba as a center of Celtic Christianity, the Abbey was destroyed by Vikings. In 1203, the Benedictines rebuilt the Abbey and continued the monastery until the Reformation. In 1938 the Iona Community, an ecumenical group, was formed and revived Columba's more natural form of spirituality.

The Iona community provides retreats for pilgrims, and holds services each morning and evening, with a daily theme, open to all. Wanting to attend a service, but deterred by the rain, Lori and I decided to save that experience for a later evening.

The next day the skies cleared and Iona's rugged beauty was bathed in sunlight. We strolled through the ancient nunnery ruins, and then on to the Abbey for a visit. I noticed covered boxes in alcoves where prayer requests for healing could be placed. Their significance would become evident when we finally attended an evening service.

Later, I walked to the other side of the island, not far from where St. Columba had originally landed so long ago. I picked up a small round stone on a pebbly beach and rolled it in my hand as I stood there reflecting on the past. Even older than St. Columba was the local legend of Finn McCool.

Our first encounter with Finn McCool's story occurred on the Giant's Causeway at the northern tip of Ireland. The legend of Finn McCool helped explain the multitude of mysterious hexagonal basalt columns that disappeared into the sea on the Antrim coast, only to reappear miles away on Scotland's Isle of Staffa. According to the story, Finn McCool built the Causeway to cross over to Scotland, to fight a Scottish giant named Benandonner. But Finn fell asleep and did not arrive, so Benendonner came across the stone footbridge looking for him. Finn's wife placed a blanket over Finn to protect him. She told the Scottish giant it was her baby son. When Benandonner saw the size of the "infant," he assumed Finn, his "father" must be truly gigantic. Benandonner ran off in fear, tearing up the Causeway behind him so Finn could not follow.

The following afternoon, the Scottish part of the story came alive for me, as I sailed with others on Captain Davie Kirkpatrick's boat, the "Iolaire of Iona," to tiny Staffa, about an hour away.

A mere half mile wide, Staffa magically appeared, its straight hexagonal columns giving rise to the grassy meadow on top. This tranquil, volcanic island was a welcome contrast to the cacophony of the crowds at the Giant's Causeway. The boat landed at a scant old mooring, where a rusted stairway led to the top, and a sea level path followed along the basaltic walls to Fingal's Cave.

Carefully negotiating the ragged rock path, I hurried to the famed sea cave, named after Finn

McCool. Once inside the dark grotto, the sound of crashing waves took me back to a time when Felix Mendelssohn stood transfixed near this same spot. At age 20, while visiting Staffa during a stormy journey, the view and sounds emanating from the cave inspired his renowned "Hebrides Overture", also known as "Fingal's Cave." A friend of his wrote at the time: "He told me how the thing came to him in its full form and color on his view of Fingal's Cave…" (The Life Of Felix Mendelssohn-Bartholdy, W.A. Lampadius, 1887, p. 92).

Sailing back through the Sound of Iona, the captain quizzed us as he negotiated a narrow channel near Mull: "Who knows what happened here?" Several passengers quickly replied, "David Balfour was shipwrecked here." "That's right," Kirkpatrick nodded, recalling the story of the classic novel, *Kidnapped*, inspired by Robert Louis Stevenson's childhood trips to the area with his father, a builder of nearby lighthouses.

After being tricked and imprisoned on a brig, Balfour washed ashore on the tiny barren islet of Erraid, right next to us. He endured several days of unwelcome solitude before discovering the low tide, which allowed him to wade across to Mull. Along with a wealthy survivor, he traversed Scotland, evading enemies and eventually returning home.

Back at the hotel that evening, we saw the two ladies from the Lake District again. They were getting ready to go back to the Abbey. We decided to join them. Equipped with flashlights, we made our way past the hotel's garden and onto the gravel road in back, for the quarter mile walk.

A golden glow emanated from the Abbey windows. About a hundred parishioners silently filed in. This evening's observance focused on prayers for healing. After hymns and scripture readings, those seeking prayers were invited to kneel on pillows arranged in a circle at the center. Leaders then stood behind them and said prayers. Afterwards, another prayer was given by a leader, reciting the names of those who had placed requests in the boxes we had noticed earlier. On other evenings, different themes included justice, peace and the integrity of creation, and creativity and commitment.

Walking back to the hotel afterwards, with the island aglow in the moonlight, and nary a sound but the crunch of gravel beneath our feet, we felt we had at last found the solitude we were seeking. The small smooth stone resting in my hand would remind me, once back home, of the peacefulness that was ours on Iona.

Devenish Island Monastic Site

Londonderry Mural

Chapter 9

St. Columba

Ireland's Other Saint

Note: The story of Iona from Chapter 6 is retold, here centered on St. Columba.

According to legend, St. Patrick drove the snakes out of Ireland. There must be something to that story. In several journeys to all corners of the Emerald Isle, I have never caught so much as a glimpse of a serpent.

However, St. Patrick's work was not as thorough when it came to demons. When he drove the demons out of his fasting place on Croagh Patrick in the fifth century, some of them went to Glencolmcille in Ireland's County Donegal and wrought havoc there for years. Then it was up to Ireland's other saint, St. Columba, to work a miracle.

My wife, Lori, and I were first introduced to St. Columba in Glencolmcille, while researching settings for her latest novel, *The Thin Place*. The Gaelic name means Valley of St. Columba. In the sixth century, Columba is said to have ministered there. Legend recalls that demons driven to Glencolmcille by St. Patrick were expelled from the valley by Columba.

On our visit, after settling in to scenic Castle Murray House in nearby Dunkineely, we trekked through the village at Glencolmcille and across the rugged hills. We followed the "Turas Cholmcille," St. Columba's fifteen station pilgrimage, which included ancient standing stones, a holy well, chapel, stone bed and wishing stone. At station 9, *Cloch na Aonaigh, "The Stone of the Gathering,"* a six foot high carved slab with a hole near the top, Lori gingerly followed tradition: "The pilgrim circles the cairn three times, praying, and then, placing his back to the stone, makes a declaration renouncing the World, the Flesh, and the Devil." Not missing a trick, she then peered through the hole hoping to "see heaven." Lastly, she called impishly to me, while putting her finger through the opening. Touching my finger to hers, we felt like the young lovers of old, sealing their engagement through the stone. If nothing else, Lori's dutiful rituals were sure to dispel any leftover demon remnants, or so we hoped.

Our encounters with the lore of St. Columba had just begun. Interspersed over the course of several research destinations, St. Columba kept popping up.

Leaving Glencolmcille, we paused in Derry to reflect on the walled city's tormented past. St. Columba is the patron saint of Derry, having established a monastery here in 540 AD. In the Bogside area in Derry we viewed a series of larger than life murals painted on buildings, depicting the violent and bloody "Troubles" between the Irish and British that started in the 1960's. They reminded us of a dispute that befell St. Columba in 561 AD, when he tried to keep a copy of a psalter claimed by his former teacher, St. Finnian. The discord led to a battle where thousands were killed. Though Columba was initially threatened with excommunication for his part leading up to the carnage, we would learn of his ultimate fate at our next destination.

Heading south, we had chosen County Fermanagh to investigate the mysterious ancient standing stone in the middle of lonely Caldragh Graveyard, a Christian burial site on Boa Island dating from the eighteenth century. Known as the Janus Stone for having an enigmatic face on both sides, the monument was pre-Christian, considered to be over two thousand years old. Yet even now, pilgrims would place coins in a cleft on top of the stone, apparently for luck. This image along with a nearby "fairy tree," a whitethorn adorned with ribbons and trinkets, have given the graveyard a reputation as a "thin place," where souls can pass between the physical and spiritual world.

Our base of operations in this southern section of Northern Ireland was the stately Manor House Hotel, a bright yellow Victorian structure set on a broad lawn overlooking Lower Loch Erne, near Kildeas. While exploring the loch on the hotel's boat, Lady of the Lake, we spotted Devenish Island, with its well preserved round tower, 100 feet tall, and monastery ruins. A visit to the island revealed that St. Molaise, a resident monk during the sixth century, played a key role in Columba's life.

After the deadly battle mentioned earlier, Columba was spared excommunication, but he agonized over the guilt that consumed him. He consulted with his soul friend and confessor, St. Moloise, who told him that to atone for the loss of life caused by his actions, Columba must leave Ireland. His mission was to save a soul for each one that had been lost in the battle.

Exiling himself to Scotland, Columba landed on Iona in 563 and founded a monastery. One theory is that the name, Iona, originated from an ancient form of "isle of Columba."

As though continuing in Columba's footsteps, we now headed to Iona for a time of reflection. The secluded isle, off Scotland's west coast, is not a place that is visited as an afterthought. Reaching Iona's Argyll Hotel requires a drive through central Scotland, two ferries, and finally a long walk from the pier, often in the rain. Nonetheless, the allure of this isolated speck of land, amidst the stark environs of the Inner Hebrides, has stirred passion in such diverse realms as ancient mythology, Celtic faith, music, literature, and contemporary pilgrimages.

That evening during dinner at the hotel, we exchanged pleasantries with two ladies at the next table. From England's Lake District, they remarked that they made an annual pilgrimage to Iona. "We keep returning for the nightly services at the Abbey," they said.

The Abbey, founded by St. Columba as a center of Celtic Christianity, was destroyed by Vikings. In 1203, the Benedictines rebuilt the Abbey and continued the monastery until the Reformation. In 1938 the Iona Community, an ecumenical Christian group, was formed and has revived the more natural form of spirituality, known as Celtic Christianity. The Iona community provides retreats for pilgrims, and holds services each morning and evening, with a daily theme, open to all.

The next day the skies were clear and Iona's rugged beauty was bathed in sunlight. We strolled through the ancient nunnery ruins, and then on to the Abbey for a visit. Back at the hotel that evening, we saw the two ladies from the Lake District again. They shared with us that the prior evening's service at the Abbey had focused on prayers of peace for the world. They were getting ready to go again, so we decided to follow. Equipped with flashlights, we made our way past the hotel's garden and onto the gravel road in back of the hotel for the quarter mile walk to the Abbey Church.

A golden glow emanated from the windows as we approached. About a hundred parishioners silently filed in and took seats. This evening's observance was a service of prayers for healing. After hymns were sung and scriptures read, those seeking prayers of healing were invited to kneel on pillows arranged in a circle at the center of the church. Leaders then stood behind them and said a prayer, moving around the circle until all had been prayed over. Then the supplicants returned to their seats while others came forward, about fifty in all that night.

Walking back to the hotel later, with the island aglow in the moonlight, and the crunch of our shoes on the gravel the only sound, we felt we had found an ideal place for contemplation, a brief respite from the busyness of our lives back home.

Even so, our research and St. Columba's exploits did not stop at Iona. In fact the most famous legend for which he has received little modern acclaim was yet to come. From Iona, he journeyed through Scotland spreading the gospel. We also left Iona for the mainland of Scotland. While relaxing at our next destination, the comfortable Loch Ness Lodge overlooking the long, narrow lake, we were surprised to learn that the folktale of the monster the loch is known for, is thought to have originated with St. Columba in 561 AD. During his mission work in the area, St. Columba happened upon a man who had just been killed by a water monster. Sending a companion onto the lake to flush out the monster, Columba was ready when the creature appeared, and gave a command, banishing the foul beast to the bottom of the loch.

Columba continued winning converts to Christianity and performing miracles. The later days of his life were spent quietly on Iona, where he died in 597AD. We returned home having found more than just the thin places we sought. We had found the remarkable story of Ireland's other saint.

Abbey Church Iona

Courtyard Abbey Church

Chapter 10

A Spiritual Interlude

*Finding renewal through the ancient witness
of Celtic Christianity*

*Note: The draw of Iona from yet another perspective,
first published in the Orange City News, January 15, 2014.*

While researching settings for her latest novel, my wife, Lori, and I followed the trail of St. Columba from his early ministry at Glencolmcille in Ireland's County Donegal, to the remote Isle of Iona, off Scotland's western coast. On Iona's barren, windswept shores, St. Columba in 563 AD established an abbey that became a center for Celtic Christianity.

While Lori's heroine was on a personal spiritual journey to sacred places cherished by her long lost love, we were on a journey of our own, seeking peaceful solitude, far from the contentious discord that had enveloped our Christian denomination. Spending a few days amidst the offerings of the Iona Community, we found renewal and a broader perspective from which to view our faith.

Iona first came to our attention thanks to Sir Kenneth Clark's monumental TV series, *Civilisation*. In the first episode, "By the Skin of Our Teeth," Clark described how western civilization survived after the fall of Rome, thanks to Irish monks on remote Atlantic coastal islands like Iona, who preserved and produced the sacred texts while barbarian hordes roamed the European continent.

Years later, we were privileged to host John Philip Newell in our home, while he was in town lecturing on Celtic Spirituality. Newell had served for several years as Warden of the Iona Abbey, which had been rebuilt by the Iona Community in 1938. From his lectures and books, such as *Listening for the Heartbeat of God*, we were heartened by the welcoming openness of Celtic Spirituality, which senses the sacred presence of God in all aspects of life and creation.

Not to be confused with new age ideas, Celtic Spirituality celebrates the triune majesty of God bringing light to all the world through the transformative power of love as expressed in the beloved apostle John's gospel.

For three days, we embraced the serenity we found on this ruggedly alluring island. In the evenings we joined with a diverse group of faith seekers at the Abbey Church for a time of singing, scripture reading and prayer. Each night of the week centered on a different theme, including prayers for those in need of healing, peace for the world, care for creation, justice, and commitment.

This Celtic style of faith flourished in the early days on the British Isles, somewhat in isolation from the rest of Europe. Unfortunately, at odds with the more structured Roman style, Celtic Christianity was cast aside at the Synod of Whitby in 664AD. As Newell writes, the faith may have been better served over the centuries had the benefits of both approaches been embraced.

Lori and I are grateful that Celtic Christian Spirituality has survived, though at the fringes, and has gained more attention in recent years. The opportunity to enrich our faith by viewing through a Celtic lens has opened us to a more accepting sensitivity to those whose Christian commitment has led them in a direction other than our own.

Gerald Herter and Companions by John Muir Wilderness

Yosemite's Half Dome from Taft Point

Chapter 11
On the Trail of John Muir
From Scotland to America and beyond

Note: A version of this chapter was first published in Celtic Life International, April 2020.

I had no idea when I enrolled at the University of Wisconsin many years ago, that I would be at the beginning of a life long journey that would often cross paths with the legacy of the adventurer and environmentalist, John Muir.

We shared a cultural heritage. Muir immigrated to the United States at the age of 10 from Scotland with his parents in 1849. My grandfather, Rex Phillips, came to America from Northern Ireland. But a couple centuries earlier, his ancestors arrived on Irish shores from Scotland.

Working on his family's farm in central Wisconsin, Muir was mostly self-taught. After eleven years, he arrived in Madison at age 22. His curious alarm clock inventions brought him there to exhibit at the state fair. One of them combined a clock, mostly whittled out of wood, that at the appointed hour, linked by levers to a bed, tipped the sleeper out in an upright position.

In Madison, Muir discovered the opportunity to study at the University of Wisconsin. Having only 77 students at the time, the campus consisted of four buildings. Muir lived and took classes in North Hall. The setting was fitting with green hills nestled beside expansive Lake Mendota.

A century later, I would walk a mile from my dormitory down the Lakeshore Path to the Old Red Gym for gymnastics practice. By then, the University boasted over 30,000 students using dozens of buildings. Along the way each day I passed by a wooded area bordering the path known as Muir Woods. At the top, Muir Knoll was dedicated in 1918, near the black locust tree where Muir received his first botany lesson. A ski jump constructed there was used for maneuvers by ROTC cadets during World War II. Though I participated in ROTC, the ski jump had long since been removed. However, an ROTC-related political science course brought me to a North Hall classroom in the late 1960's.

Known to be a pacifist, Muir would most likely not have been drawn to ROTC, though the program was conceived during the 1860's. While available for the draft, Muir's name was never called for Civil War duty.

Only picking classes that interested him, Muir studied chemistry, math, physics, Greek, Latin, botany and geology, but did not complete the requirements for a degree. (Later in life he would be awarded honorary degrees both from the University of Wisconsin and Harvard University). Nevertheless, mixed emotions filled his thoughts as he reflected upon his departure:

"From the top of a hill on the north side of Lake Mendota I gained a last wistful, lingering view of the beautiful University grounds and buildings where I had spent so many hungry and happy and hopeful days. There with streaming eyes I bade my blessed Alma Mater farewell. But I was only leaving one University for another, the Wisconsin University for the University of the Wilderness." (*The Story of My Boyhood and Youth*, John Muir, 1913).

Muir's early wanderings focused on his love for botany, studying and collecting numerous specimens. During the following two years working on a sawmill and factory in Canada, a trek through a swamp revealed to Muir the rare and lovely *Calypso borealis*, a white orchid "of the utmost simple purity like a snowflower." That discovery led to his first published essay describing the flower and setting, including the famous quote: "It seems wonderful that so frail and lovely a plant has such power over human hearts." (*The Life and Letters of John Muir,* William Frederic Bade, 1924).

A couple years after leaving Canada, Muir's first major solo hike from Louisville, Kentucky to Cedar Key, Florida, was chronicled in his book, *A Thousand Mile Walk to the Gulf* (1916). Following a similar route four years after my graduation from the University of Wisconsin, but in the far more comfortable and sporty confines of an MGB GT, my new bride, Lori, joined me for our honeymoon travels from Chicago to the Florida Keys. (Muir's adventure actually began from his Wisconsin home and passed through Chicago, before taking a train from Indianapolis to Louisville where he began the walk).

Along the way, we marveled like Muir at the vastness of Mammoth Cave in Kentucky. Muir arrived there at the end of the first week of his journey. How different it must have been. The cave was already well known at the time. There had been tours there since 1816, albeit much more rustic and crude than Lori and I would experience. In the early days, slaves were the tour guides and there was just one short or long tour. Now there are around 20 different offerings, from easy going to extremely strenuous.

As Muir described it, "Arrived at the great Mammoth Cave. I was surprised to find it in so complete naturalness...were it not for the narrow trail that leads down the glen to its door, one would not know that it had been visited."

At over 400 miles of known passages, Mammoth Cave is the longest known cave system in the world. The natural "door" remains much as it was, albeit adapted with a pathway more suited for modern visitors. The surroundings have also been developed to accommodate the growing crowds. Even in Muir's day, manmade amenities marred the setting in his view: "I never before saw Nature's grandeur in so abrupt contrast with paltry artificial gardens. The fashionable hotel grounds are in exact parlor taste, with many a beautiful plant cultivated to deformity, and arranged in strict geometrical beds, the whole pretty affair a laborious failure side by side with Divine beauty."

Missing the main section of the Appalachian Mountain range that was to become Great Smoky

Mountains National Park, Muir's southerly route through Tennessee and the southwest corner of North Carolina traversed the Cumberland Mountains section. We drove in the National Park which was established in the 1930's, up to the highest point of 6,643 feet at Clingmans Dome, and around the historic structures of Cades Cove, gaining a feel for the demanding terrain Muir had to negotiate, as well as the quaint houses and farms he visited seeking food and shelter when on his route. Many a night he roughed it with only the canopy of the woods over his head.

Proceeding across Georgia, Muir stopped in coastal Savannah, where graves in the Bonaventure Cemetery served as his accommodation for the night. With each of us having cousins in Savannah, Lori and I found far more inviting lodgings when staying there over the years.

Muir's multi-state walk concluded in northwest Florida's Cedar Key. Though our furthest destination was Key West, our sojourn nearer Cedar Key at Orlando's recently opened Walt Disney World, most likely would have generated head scratching dismay from Muir, had he witnessed what humans had wrought from a central Florida swampland.

Muir's original plan from Florida was to catch a ship bound for South America, whereupon he would find the headstreams of the Amazon and follow it all the way to the ocean. Only later would he realize that his disappointment at not locating such a ship would turn out to be a blessing. While in the swampy southeastern reaches of the United States, he had contracted malaria, leaving him laid up for several months. Not improving after a month's stay in Cuba, he felt the need to leave the sub-tropical climate.

His next goal was the North American West. Getting there first required a voyage to New York where the ships for the West coast departed. The brief stopover in New York City was not to Muir's liking with its crowds of people and concrete jungle of buildings. He was anxious for the wilds where he thrived. The cooler climate did help restore his health.

From New York, Muir's ship landed in Panama, where a rail journey brought him across the isthmus to the Pacific for the final sea leg of the journey. His 6-hour traverse was faster than what Lori and I experienced on our cruise ship through the Panama Canal. The Canal was not completed until 1914. However, the comforts of our ship left us with little sense of the nineteenth century quest felt by Muir.

With Muir's arrival in California, the most storied part of his life began. Pausing but a day in San Francisco, he headed east on foot to Yosemite. Having a similar desire to be closer to the grandeurs of the far west, Lori and I left our Chicago home four years after getting married, and drove to southern California, never looking back. Over the next forty plus years, we followed Muir's footsteps across the High Sierra and beyond.

Muir's first trip to Yosemite covered about 300 miles and took the better part of two months. Of his initial impressions of Yosemite, Muir wrote little compared to later descriptions. In a letter to a dear friend dated July 26, 1868 he summed up his feelings, "I thought of you, Mrs. Carr, when I was in the glorious Yosemite…It is by far the grandest of all of the special temples of Nature I was ever permitted to enter. It must be the sanctum sanctorum of the Sierras."

The first view of Yosemite Valley for Lori and I was one that many visitors will remember and never forget. Our first summer in California, we drove to Yosemite. Immediately upon exiting the long, dark Wawona Tunnel, approaching the park from the south, our senses were stunned by the spectacular panorama of the dramatically massive cliffs and main valley of Yosemite. With the sheer granite of 3,000 foot El Capitan on the left, radiant Bridalveil Falls flowing in slender majesty for over 600 feet on the right, and iconic Half Dome, looming at over 4,700 feet high in the distant center, one's jaw could not help but drop in genuine awe.

In Muir's following year upon returning to Yosemite he wrote, "[T]he far-famed valley came suddenly into view throughout almost its whole extent. The noble walls--sculptured into endless variety of domes and gables, spires and battlements and plain mural precipices--all a-tremble with the thunder tones of the falling water. The level bottom seemed to be dressed like a garden, --sunny meadows here and there, and groves of pine and oak; the river of Mercy sweeping in majesty through the midst of them and flashing back the sunbeams. The great Tissiack, or Half-Dome, rising at the upper end of the valley to a height of nearly a mile, is nobly proportioned and life-like, the most impressive of all the rocks, holding the eye in devout admiration, calling it back again and again from falls or meadows, or even the mountains beyond, --marvelous cliffs, marvelous in sheer dizzy depth and sculpture, types of endurance. Thousands of years have they stood in the sky exposed to rain, snow, frost, earthquake and avalanche, yet they still wear the bloom of youth." (*My First Summer in the Sierra*, John Muir, 1911)

My mind is boggled at the thought that as I gaze on the magnificent Yosemite Valley today, the view of the massive rock formations and waterfalls appear just as they did for John Muir a century ago. Though he would have lamented the overcrowding of the Valley that speaks to the park's current popularity, I am sure Muir would have concurred that the eminent stature of the natural formations remains as solid as the granite that forms the valley walls.

As part of my first summer trip to Yosemite in 1977, while driving along the east side of the magnificent Sierra Nevada Mountains, I could see the pinnacles of Mount Whitney as we passed by. Mt. Whitney, at 14, 505 feet in altitude, is North America's highest peak south of Alaska. I remembered a summer as a teenager, when I traveled with a group to Rocky Mountain National Park. We hiked to the top of 14,255 foot Long's Peak, the highest in that park. I wondered how Mt. Whitney would compare.

Though the widely traveled Muir never saw Colorado, he became the inspiration of Enos Mills, who would later become known as the father of Rocky Mountain National Park. Stemming from a chance encounter with Muir on a San Francisco beach in 1889, Mills became a staunch advocate for preserving nature. Having ascended Long's Peak hundreds of times himself, alone and as a guide, Mills was the driving force that led to the establishment of Rocky Mountain National Park in 1915.

Though missing out on Long's Peak, Muir conquered many peaks in his day. In October, 1873, he was one of the earliest to reach the summit of Mt. Whitney. Two years later, Muir was the first to ascend what is now known as the Mountaineer's route.

By the summer of 1979, two colleagues and I finally decided to tackle Mt. Whitney. At that time, we knew nothing about backpacking, or hiking at high altitudes. We were terribly out of shape. But off we went. What was supposed to be a 20 hike to the top of Mount Whitney turned into a 45-mile death march! As we hiked out to the trail head almost half dead and never having made it to the top of the mountain, we swore we would never do that again.

It would be another thirteen years before we returned and finally made the summit, using the same route. Muir contrasted his Mountaineer route (denoted as Class 3 in mountain climbing terms) with our Class 1 "mule" hiking route: "But for climbers there is a canyon which comes down from the north shoulder of the Whitney peak. Well-seasoned limbs will enjoy the climb of 9000 feet required by this direct route. But soft, succulent people should go the mule way." (Century Magazine, November, 1891).

Even so, by then we had been seasoned by a series of annual treks during the intervening years, inspired by that initial ill-fated attempt at Mt. Whitney. Beginning with a hike over the same High Sierra Kearsarge Pass trod by Muir, we proceeded to such Muir favorites as Sequoia, King's Canyon and Grand Canyon National Parks, as well as several forays into the backcountry of Yosemite. A year after Muir's death in 1914, construction of a trail in his name began. Upon completion in 1938, the John Muir Trail covered 211 miles from Mt. Whitney to the heart of Yosemite, traversing some of the High Sierra locales most revered by Muir. Over 80 miles of the trail have been covered by my colleagues and I so far, in various segments over the years.

That a lover of mountains would also be fascinated by the vastness of the Grand Canyon is not surprising. As Muir put it "Deep canyons attract like high mountains; the deeper they are, the more surely are we drawn into them". Like most of us, he struggled to describe the Canyon's unique character: "try as I may, not in the least sparing myself, I cannot tell the hundredth part of the wonders of its features." (Steep Trails, John Muir, 1918). Nevertheless, over two dozen pages of an article in 1902, he proceeded to elaborate in exquisite detail all aspects of the canyons expansive natural magnificence, including flora, fauna and early native dwellers, along with the striking geologic proportions.

Muir's advice for taking in the fullness of the Canyon was that "The trip down and up can be made afoot easily in a day...But all who have time should go prepared to camp awhile on the riverbank, to rest and learn something about the plants and animals and the mighty flood roaring past." (Steep Trails).

In the course of a half dozen treks to the canyon floor, I am sure that the rustic facilities I found still offered more comforts than the "good spacious camp-ground in a mesquite grove" by the river, that Muir encountered. At age seventeen, I applied his first suggestion, hiking in and out in one day, stopping at the bottom just long enough for a cool swim in the murky green water of a swimming pool that has long since been filled in with dirt and vegetation.

Thirty years later with my two colleagues, we hiked rim to rim, camping at the bottom in a fashion more attuned to Muir's approach. Subsequent visits included stays with beds and meals at rustic Phantom Ranch, as well as two trips rafting through the Canyon on the Colorado River. We could never get enough of this natural wonder of the world.

Along with his many adventures, the other place that kept drawing Muir back was Alaska. Starting with his first trip in 1879, Muir would travel to Alaska seven times over the following twenty years.

One of Muir's motivations for studying the Alaska wilderness relates back to the origins of Yosemite. From his extensively documented explorations of Yosemite, he developed a thoughtful and detailed theory of the geologic history of the region. His observations of such features as the U-shaped valleys, and the grooved and polished rock formations convinced Muir that glaciation had been at work: "[I]n my opinion future investigation will uncover proofs of the existence in the earlier ages of Sierra Nevada ice, of vast glaciers which flowed to the very foot of the range." ("*Yosemite Glaciers*," New York Tribune, December 5, 1871).

Surprisingly, the renowned geologist of the time dismissed Muir's theory as absurd, contending that the cause was stream erosion coupled with fault upheavals. He looked upon Muir as a young, undereducated "sheepherder," referring to Muir's means of support while in Yosemite. Nonetheless, an official geologic study released in 1930 revealed that Muir's theory was substantially correct. Though there were several separate periods of glaciation with stream erosion at work in between, the bulk of the valley's features were found to be the result of the glaciers.

While most of the glaciers in Yosemite were gone or in rapid retreat as the nineteenth century wore on, Muir found in Alaska much younger glacial action in progress. Numerous formations appeared much like Muir would have expected in Yosemite eons earlier.

Muir was credited with rediscovering Glacier Bay on that 1879 trip. He traveled with native guides and a missionary, S. Hall Young, who recalled in his autobiography, suggesting that "the greatest of all the glaciers" they encountered should be named for Muir, which it subsequently was. (*Hall Young of Alaska, The Mushing Parson, p. 204).*

In years following, Muir Glacier would become the highlight for a growing throng of tourists drawn to

Glacier Bay as a result of Muir's and Young's vivid accounts of this newly accessible wilderness.

Alas, by the time Lori and I made our way to Glacier Bay a hundred years later (by way of a cushy cruise ship), the grand Muir Glacier had all but disappeared, having shrunk to the point that it no longer reached the Bay, but resided back among the mountain recesses. In order to get a sense of its earlier grandeur, our ship pulled up close to nearby Margerie Glacier, whose massive mile-wide front on the Bay, rising 250 feet from the water's edge, was comparable to what Muir Glacier looked like in Muir's time.

Glacier Bay has witnessed rapid retreat of its glaciers in less than 300 years. At the height of the Little Ice Age in 1759, the whole Bay was covered by one huge glacier. By Muir's day, the ice had already receded by almost 50 miles. Today, the Bay extends more than 65 miles inward.

Muir's exploits in Alaska also revealed the fearless explorer that he was, risking his own life and saving others. In his book, *Alaska Days with John Muir*, Young describes in vivid detail how amazingly passionate and fearless Muir was. In admiration, Young remarked "I began to recognize him as my Master who was to lead me into enchanting regions of beauty and mystery, which without his aid must forever have remained unseen by the eyes of my soul."

Young was soon to learn first-hand of Muir's prowess. On his first hike with Muir, he marveled "Then Muir began to slide up that mountain. I had been with mountain climbers before, but never one like him.

A deer-lope over the smoother slopes, a sure instinct for the easiest way into a rocky fortress, an instant and unerring attack, a serpent-glide up the steep; eye, hand and foot all connected dynamically; with no appearance of weight to his body."

Young struggled his best to keep up with Muir, but near the top Young took a tumble and was hanging precariously from a cliff when Muir came to his rescue: "Hold fast; I'm going to get you out of this…Then I felt a careful hand on my back, fumbling with the waistband of my pants, my vest and shirt, gathering all in a firm grip…He drew me close to him by crooking his arm and as my head came up past his level he caught me by my collar with his teeth!… How he did it, I know not. The miracle grows as I ponder it. The wall was almost perpendicular and smooth. My weight on his jaws dragged him outwards. And yet, holding me by his teeth as a panther her cub and clinging like a squirrel to a tree, he climbed with me straight up ten or twelve feet, with only the help of my iron-shod feet scrambling on the rock. It was utterly impossible, yet he did it!"

Not only were humans the beneficiary of Muir's fearlessness. On a later foray with a faithful dog named Stickeen, not only did Muir successfully jump over a dangerously wide and deep crevasse, but he cajoled the more cautious and sensible canine to follow him, ultimately grabbing hold when the dog made his desperate leap, pulling him to safety.

The origins of Muir's adventurous athletic abilities were revealed when he wrote about his childhood in Dunbar, Scotland, on the coast just east of Edinburgh: "The roof of our house, as well as the crags and walls of the old [Dunbar] castle, offered fine mountaineering exercise." Returning to Scotland more than fifty years later, Muir had to see his childhood home again to "judge what sort of adventure getting on its roof must have been, and with all my after experience in mountaineering, I found that what I had done in daring boyhood was now beyond my skill."

By his letters, Muir expressed how thoroughly he enjoyed his homecoming, both the many relatives and friends, as well as the natural allure of the land. He spoke of his hometown, "beautifully located on a plateau above the sea and with a background of beautiful hills and dales," and of spending with a fascinating new acquaintance "the most wonderful night as far as humanity is concerned I ever had in the world…and now I am a Scotchman and at home again."

Muir reminisced that "Edinburgh is, apart from its glorious historical associations, far the most beautiful town I ever saw. I cannot conceive how it could be more beautiful. In the very heart of it rises the great Castle hill, glacier-sculptured and wild like a bit of Alaska in the midst of the most beautiful architecture to be found in the world." From there, much like a tourist, he went "by coach and boat, by the Trossachs and Loch Katrine, thence through Loch Lomond and the mountains to a railroad and on to this charming Oban."

Likewise entranced by Edinburgh, Lori and I followed a similar route, albeit driving by car, across Scotland to Oban, where we caught a ferry to the Island of Mull, and then another ferry to the captivating Isle of Iona, for a few days of retreat.

Iona is known as the birthplace of Celtic Spirituality, with an abbey first established by St. Columba in the sixth century. Muir espoused a spirituality akin to the Celtic style, which celebrates the presence of the divine essence in all creatures and aspects of the natural world. Having been raised by a strict Presbyterian minister, Muir's solid foundation in Christianity was broadened and came to be exuberantly expressed as he saw the hand of God working in nature. For example, one time upon gazing the brilliant first rays of the morning sun on an Alaskan mountaintop, he gushed "We have met with God...He sent us to his most glorious exhibition. Praise God from whom all blessings flow."

A comparable sentiment was expressed by Muir, who in later years battled to prevent Hetch Hetchy, the "other" Yosemite Valley, from being flooded to provide water for San Francisco: "Dam Hetch Hetchy! As well dam for water tanks the people's cathedrals and churches, for no holier temple has ever been consecrated by the heart of man." (*The Yosemite*, John Muir, 1912)

Though Muir was to lose that decade-long battle to save Hetch Hetchy, he built a legacy for conservation and preservation of lands filled with unique natural wonders. During his life and thereafter, he was directly responsible for the establishment of a number of American national parks and monuments. An escorted camping tour that Muir gave President Theodore Roosevelt through Yosemite in 1903 helped influence Roosevelt's decisions for creating several national parks. Muir was also co-founder and first president of the Sierra Club, which preserves and continues Muir's legacy. I am indebted to the Sierra Club, of which Lori and I are members, for the website the Club maintains, providing a wealth of information and writings by and about John Muir.

Part 3 – Wales

Cardiff Castle

Tintern Abbey

Chapter 12
Wales' Moment in the Sun
Cardiff goes all out for world leaders

Note: A version of this chapter was first published in Celtic Life International, February 2015.

Prior to the September NATO summit, Wales was, for many, just the little known appendage attached to the side of England. Surprisingly, the Welsh people lay claim to a colorful and violent past. Yet unlike the drama that has characterized Scotland and Northern Ireland lately, Wales in recent times has proved to be the more stable member of the United Kingdom.

Determined to welcome the world with a display of pride and confidence, the people of Wales came well prepared for their brief moment in the spotlight.

Two days before the NATO world leaders' dinner at Cardiff Castle, my wife, Lori, and I were enjoying tea in the seventh floor lounge of the Hilton Hotel across the street. From the broad lounge windows, we felt like we could almost reach out and touch the striking 11th century castle looming large in the sunlight.

But what stood out even more from our vantage point were the ever present police in their striking yellow vests. On the sidewalk patrolmen strode in pairs at 50 yard intervals. On the street, motor cycle teams of six zoomed by every few minutes, as well as frequent squad cars and troopers on horseback. Officers peered out from atop the castle tower, while their colleagues swarmed the grounds like bright ants among the tourists.

When we planned our trip to Wales nine months earlier, we had no idea our visit would coincide with the summit of the 28 NATO country leaders. Even as we toured the castle's ornate banqueting hall earlier in the afternoon, the guide made no mention that the likes of President Barack Obama, British Prime Minister David Cameron, and German Chancellor Angela Merkel would soon gather for a historic meal in this storied room.

Our peaceful afternoon tea was disrupted suddenly as three vested police officers strode into the hotel lounge, metal detectors in hand. They proceeded to meticulously screen around every chair and above each ceiling tile for nefarious devices. Like all the police we encountered in Cardiff that week, these were a friendly, yet professional bunch, hailing from all parts of Britain. "There are ten thousand of us here," one from Herefordshire mentioned proudly. I asked who was minding their hometowns while they were here. "Other officers are called upon to step up," he replied matter-of-factly.

Later we walked down by the waterfront, which the Welsh have developed into a bustling center for tourist activity. The modern Millennium Center and slate-covered National Assembly Building stood out next to classical structures, like the red brick Pierhead building that reflected Wales' maritime past.

Lori spotted an attractive pin in a tiny gift shop nearby that she had to have. We sensed excitement in the sales clerk's voice as we talked with her. "The warships are starting to come in. Have you seen them by the dock?" She pointed toward the left side of the harbor, behind a historic Norwegian church built for sailors a couple centuries ago. "President Obama will be spending his nights on one of the ships during the NATO Summit." She was looking forward to having a great vantage point watching for him, since her apartment was on the top floor of a building overlooking the harbor. She also alerted us to various security measures, such as street closings and a complete planned shutdown and rebooting of all area computer networks just before the Summit.

When we got to the dock, a hundred people crowded the fence in front of the first British warship to arrive, while a reporter and cameraman broadcasted the news. We observed added security measures. Small boats laden with police dotted the harbor. Along with foot and motorcycle police patrols, now there were also pairs of military types with assault weapons watching vigilantly.

"Cardiff must be the safest place to be this week," I mentioned to Lori as we returned to our hotel. Stepping out of the elevator at our floor, yet another policeman, seated by the door keeping watch, greeted us as we walked by.

"Since the Summit starts tomorrow, we had better leave early to avoid the expected traffic delays," Lori suggested. I agreed as I consulted the map. Our planned driving route, on the M4 motorway up toward Tintern Abbey, passed close to nearby Newport, the site of the Summit meetings at the Celtic Manor Resort.

We held our breath the next morning, but managed to avoid street closures and the protestors anticipated by the castle. Even so, we knew our presence was observed along the motorway. On every overpass between Cardiff and Newport, police closely eyed all vehicles moving by.

Turning at last onto the local road that led to the Wye River Valley, we breathed a sigh of relief. The peaceful, bucolic charm of this scenic rural corner of Wales proved a welcome contrast to the armed camp atmosphere in Cardiff. I could almost feel Wordsworth's sense of joy as he once wrote near Tintern Abbey:

Of aspect more sublime; that blessed mood,
In which the burthen of the mystery,
In which the heavy and the weary weight
Of all this unintelligible world

Is lighten'd:—that serene and blessed mood,
In which the affections gently lead us on,
…when the fretful stir
Unprofitable, and the fever of the world,
Have hung upon the beatings of my heart,
How oft, in spirit, have I turned to thee
O sylvan Wye! Thou wanderer through the wood
How often has my spirit turned to thee!

Set amongst rolling green hills, the extensive 12th century Abbey ruins exuded a silent strength even now. A walk through the remaining gothic structures, their past grandeur described on aptly placed plaques, helped us grasp the extent of the sophisticated community that flourished here so long ago.

We continued along the Wye River to the sumptuous Llangoed Hall, a country house hotel, our home for the next two nights. Once owned by the husband of Laura Ashley, the hotel is richly furnished with fabrics from her collection. Well attended to by watchful servants, we could now relax in the serene countryside of Wales.

But one last reminder of the NATO Summit remained. We noticed that several of the parking spots in front of the hotel were reserved for the UAE. Upon querying the staff, we were told that the United Arab Emirates representatives to the Summit were staying at Llangoed Hall.

The following day after a walk by the Wye River behind the hotel, we turned on the TV in time to see President Obama speaking as he readied to depart. "Let me begin by thanking my great friend, Prime Minister Cameron -- and his entire team -- for hosting this NATO Summit and making it such a success. And I want to thank the people of Newport and Cardiff and the people of Wales for welcoming me and my delegation so warmly. It's a great honor to be the first sitting U.S. President to visit Wales...Thank you very much, people of Wales. I've had a wonderful time."

We were pleased for our new found friends, the Welsh people. They had done themselves proud and shown the world and us genuine hospitality.

Llangorse Lake Crannog

Castell Henllys

Chapter 13
Discovering Wales' Ancient Sites
Mysteries of the past off the beaten track

Note: A version of this chapter was first published in Celtic Life International, October 2015.

"Come join us," the amiable man with a Welsh accent waved from across the farmer's field. My wife, Lori, and I soon learned he was Bernard Owen from Safari Tours, escorting a couple to the prehistoric burial chamber at Capel Gorman in the heart of Snowdonia.

We were staying nearby at charming Tan-y-Foel Country House. Proprietor, Ria Smith, had directed us to this out of the way monument. Just a couple miles drive along a narrow country road led us to the spot, where a small sign designated the 4,000 year old site's location. We gladly joined the threesome, which included Owen's friends, shopkeepers from Llandudno, who he had been coaxing for some time to visit the lesser known gems in Snowdonia.

We were soon to discover what few travelers to this enchanting part of the United Kingdom ever do. Sure, the mystical presence of England's Stonehenge is known worldwide. Moreover, thousands vie annually in a lottery to be on hand at Ireland's

Newgrange for daybreak of the winter solstice, as the sun's first rays penetrate to the core of the Neolithic passage tomb.

But what of Wales' ancient treasures? They are numerous, but take a little more effort to find. For those who take the time, a rich history is revealed, along with the scenic charm of Wales' pastoral backroads.

Our journey had started in Cardiff. After exploring the castle and other crowded tourist attractions in the city, we longed for the peaceful solitude of the lush countryside. We did not have to go far to reach our first encounter with Megalithic Wales. Tinkinswood Burial Chamber, just a few miles southwest of Cardiff in the Vale of Glamorgan, proved to be an excellent place for an introduction to the ancient culture. Except for one local couple, we had the site to ourselves.

Tinkinswood embodies a number of common elements found in several sites we were to visit over the following days. First the burial chamber shared a field with cows and sheep, which resided in oblivious disinterest to the primordial significance of the ground on which they grazed. They barely looked up as we strode by. Farmers are required by law to allow visitors to traverse their fields for access to the sites.

This type of burial chamber is known as a portal tomb or dolmen. Dating back 6,000 years to the Neolithic period, Tinkinswood consists of a 40 ton limestone capstone measuring 24 feet across, suspended by several large upright stones. When used in earlier times, the structure was covered by a mound of earth, much like the reconstructed Newgrange is today.

We walked beneath the capstone, where hundreds of human bones were found during excavation. The tomb is all that remains of a prehistoric village's residents, whose existence left many untold mysteries, such as how they managed to erect the massive capstone.

Perhaps from this lack of recorded history, or from the tradition of oral history, the ancient sites are focal points for folk tales and legends. Tinkinswood has a couple ill-fated ones. A person who spends the night on one of three special days of the year will die, go mad, or become a poet. Also, dancing here on the Sabbath can have dire consequences, as a group of ladies purportedly found out. A collection of boulders to the south of the chamber are thought to be all that's left of them.

What makes this site especially desirable for first time visitors are the prerecorded audio messages. They tell the story of the ancient people who once lived here. We turned a crank to generate the electrical current that drives the audio player. Four separate audio selections covered the Neolithic Period, the tomb builders, building a tomb, and further exploration.

Another smaller burial chamber of similar structure, St. Lythans, lies about a mile away. A walk following a stretch of the Millennium Heritage Trail connects the two sites. We were content to observe St. Lythans from the road before moving on.

Heading north, we stopped briefly at Llangorse Lake in Brecon Beacons National Park to take in the crannog there. While some ancient lake dwellings date as far back as the Neolithic period of Tinkinwoods, the Llangorse Crannog was built around 916 AD.

A crannog is a defensive dwelling built out on a lake. Common in Ireland and Scotland, Llangorse Crannog is the only known one in Wales. The remains of the actual crannog form a small, currently uninhabited island 40 meters from shore.

We viewed the crannog from a platform extending out from the water's edge, where the government service, Cadw, maintains an authentic reconstruction at the Welsh Crannog Center. White swans swam close by to observe our movements. Inside and around the conical, thatched roof structure, we read displays of the life and legends from the time the crannog was active. Apparently built for a royal household, bits of history suggest a tragic end, when a king's wife and dozens of others were killed by a Saxon army.

Continuing on our journey north, we eventually reached Snowdonia and settled in for a few days near Betws-y-Coed, at Tan-y-Foel Country House. Luckily the next morning, Ria gave us specific driving directions to Capel Gorman, where we had met the aforementioned Bernard Owen, a seasoned veteran of Celtic history.

As we were beginning to realize, finding the lesser known sites can be a challenge along the narrow, poorly marked lanes of rural Wales. So when Owen recommended we check out another intriguing spot, Fairy Glen, we gladly accepted his offer to follow behind his van. Soon we were driving along a lushly overgrown wood, beside a narrow ravine. Fairy Glen is known more for its mystical scenic beauty than for specific fairy sightings.

Stopping to peer down the Glen's shallow gorge, Owen instructed us to look closely. There almost hidden amongst greenery covering all sides was an ancient stone bridge spanning the brief chasm. Though the main part of Fairy Glen is reached by a footpath out of Betwys-y-Coed, Owen had brought us to a magical remote section with a centuries old bridge few visitors would see.

Ready to continue our search for vestiges of the Neolithic era, we waved good by to Owen and his guests and drove to the Isle of Anglesey, just north of Snowdonia across the Menai Strait. Here the fine passage tomb of Bryn Celli Dhu revealed more glimpses into the lives of early Welsh inhabitants.

The walk to the sight required navigating several lengthy stretches of hedgerow-enclosed pathways that zigzagged along, ending with a strategically placed kissing gate (so named, not for the more amorous implications, but for a unique design allowing one person to pass at a time, but not livestock. The swinging gate touches or "kisses" each side of the enclosure but is not latched to either side).

The long walk proved worthwhile, when Bryn Celli Dhu came into view. Aptly named, meaning the "mound in the dark grove," the portal tomb was buried under a mound of grass-covered earth, much like it would have been thousands of years ago.

The sun produced sharp shadows as we entered the 28 foot long chamber. On a cleft inside were trinkets, including a doll, feathers, fruit, a shaft of wheat, and a fork. No doubt these were from a modern day recreation of an ancient ritual. Outside, remnants of a stone circle, or henge, are evident, forming a ditch around the monument. A unique carving found near a ceremonial pit is known as the "Pattern Stone" for its winding serpentine decorations.

The immediate area of the mound is fenced to protect from nearby grazing livestock. Plaques on the fence describe the burial chamber and henge. For Anglesey, another unique aspect of Bryn Celli Dhu is the alignment of the chamber. The configuration is designed to catch the sun's rays throughout the length of the tomb at daybreak on the summer solstice, as contrasted to Newgrange which was constructed for the same purpose, but aligned for the winter solstice.

Like other ancient sites, there were more cows than people in the vicinity of Bryn Celli Dhu. While a few more people were touring the Bronze Age copper mines on the nearby Great Orme headland next to

Llandudno, the more popular attraction appeared to be the tramway and the Summit Complex it served at the top of the limestone promontory. Visitors marveled at the sea view and exhibits while dining at the restaurant facility. Again, we sought out the quieter corners, this time in the cavities of the earth.

The copper mines are an extensive labyrinth of tunnels dating back 4,000 years. We descended deep into the excavated hillside formation, originally dug out with stone hammers and animal bones during the Bronze Age. Estimated to have been worked for a thousand years, the mines then lay dormant until reopened in Roman and more recent times. The vastness of the workings attests to the extent of the metal resources and the widespread trade economy that thrived so long ago as a result.

With our next historic destination in the southwest of Wales, we proceeded forward, stopping for a breather overnight by the beach at coastal Aberwytswh. While there we drove through scenic Rheidol Valley to Devil's Bridge. We were thinking that we might find clues relevant also to the history of the unmarked bridge at Fairy Glen. That we did and then some.

Devil's Bridge is an amazing amalgam of three bridges from three different ages, each one built atop the other. While visible from the road, a steep rocky path through the wooded vale led to even more spectacular views of waterfalls created by the river flowing under the bridges.

The topmost bridge is practically new at a little more than a hundred years of age. The highway uses this one. Beneath it, the second bridge dates to the 1750's. However, the oldest and bottom most bridge, which bears a resemblance to the one at Fairy Glen, carries the most colorful origin. Thought by legend to have been created by the Devil, himself, to trick unsuspecting peasants, the more likely builders were eleventh century monks, from nearby Strata Florida. We surmised that the Fairy Glen bridge dated from the same era.

Continuing south to Pembrokeshire Coast National Park, we returned to the Iron Age at Castell Henllys, which translates from the Welsh as "castle of the old court." Originally an early hill fort, the site now boasts an excellent reconstruction on the ancient foundations, including four large roundhouses and a granary. Based on its size, as many as 150 people may have lived here in the several thatched roof structures supported by "wattle and daub" walls and fireplaces. Considered a well defended enclave on a hill, various protective techniques were employed, such as the strategically placed upright stones that would slow and snag attackers, making them vulnerable to the inhabitants.

As contrasted to many of the remote historic sites, Castell Henllys is complete with visitor center and gift shop. The excavation and authentic re-creation makes the site popular for archeology training, school children visits, and ritual reenactments.

Just a little further on in Pembrokeshire is Pentre Ifan, considered the best preserved Neolithic burial chamber. "Ivans Village," as it translates, is striking, standing out fully exposed on a hill. I easily walked under the capstone that was suspended eight foot in the air, though some may have questioned the wisdom of lingering beneath a 16 ton, 16 foot long boulder, delicately balanced on three other stones. Considering that the mammoth stone has remained serenely suspended for over 3,500 years, I felt the odds were in my favor.

This monument has the distinction of being one of only three in Wales to have first been protected by the Ancient Monuments Protection Act of 1882. Though burial pits were found beneath the dolmen, no bones were located. The legends for this site tell of different uses, such as for child-like fairies dressed as soldiers, or being held for initiation within the site, which was supposedly enclosed at the time.

Our final ancient site on this circular swing through Wales carried a legendary name. Arthur's Stone sits high on the Cefn Bryn ridge near Reynoldston, along the scenic Gower Peninsula of South Wales. An easy path leads up the open field to the perch of the predominant stone, which commands a sweeping view down to the Bristol Channel of the Irish Sea in the distance.

Yet another of the Neolithic burial chambers protected by the Ancient Monuments Protection Act of 1882, and dating back to 2,500 B.C., Arthur's Stone's principal feature is the 25 ton, eight foot high capstone. Measuring 13 feet long by 8 feet wide, the capstone is supported just above the ground by several relatively small boulders. Deposited during the last Ice Age, this structure is thought to have been created by digging out soil beneath the capstone while inserting the supporting standing stones.

A number of legends surround this site, the main one drawing from the capstone's shape, which is much like a huge "pebble." King Arthur was said to have tossed a pebble he found in his shoe. Travelling some seven miles before landing at this spot, the stone grew from having been touched by the king, and was lifted up out of admiration by the adjoining local stones. A ten ton chunk lying next to Arthur's Stone gave rise to a legend that it was struck off the main stone by the sword of St. David, patron saint of Wales, who deplored the druid worship here. Finally, young druid maidens were known to test the faithfulness of their beloved by making a cake offering and then circling the Stone three times on hands and knees. If their intended appeared before they finished, they knew he would be a faithful husband.

Having completed our circuit of Wales in search of the ancient monuments, we ended up back near Cardiff. Two fitting attractions that can help bring perspective either before or after this journey are St. Fagans Natural History Museum, just outside of Cardiff, and the National Museum downtown. St. Fagans, in a rural village-like setting, is an outdoor reconstruction of dwellings in Wales' past. Though most are from recent centuries, there is a Celtic village re-creation that provides context from the ancient era. The National Museum takes history back to the geologic creation of Wales and follows the ancient story forward in an exhibit titled "The Evolution of Wales."

Fairy Glen Bridge

Bridge at Llanwrst

Chapter 14

Hidden Gems of Llywelyn the Great's Snowdonia

A treasure trove of history

Note: A version of this chapter was first published in Celtic Life International, June 2017.

Driving the narrow, twisty lane out from Trefriw in northern Wales, I doubted that the quality of the crude track had improved much in eight hundred years. Llywelyn the Great, Lord of Snowdonia, traversed up this wooded hill in the twelfth century when visiting Llanrhychwyn Church, since then known as Llywelyn's Church. Founded in the 6th century by Welsh Prince, Rhychwyn, nothing remains of the earliest structure. But with parts of the current building dating to the early twelfth century, the church is considered the oldest in Wales still offering services to this day.

My wife, Lori, and I were exploring historic, but out of the way places in the vicinity of the popular Snowdonia village of Betws-y-Coed. Knowledgeable Bernard Owen, local villager and owner of Snowdonia Safaris, was our guide for the day. Having chanced upon Owen during a previous visit to the Capel Gorman monolithic portal tomb, we were impressed by his breadth of knowledge centered on the area's ancient sites.

Owen had picked us up at our local accommodation, the charming Tan-y-foel Country House Bed & Breakfast, set in the serenely scenic hills of the Conwy River Valley, a couple miles above the quaint community of Llanrwst. After tea and conversation with our gracious hosts, Ria Smith and Chris Dossi, we were ready to set out. By the end of the day, this part of Wales would hold new meaning for us, as we gained a brief glimpse into the distant past, where Llywelyn the Great and others from his House of Aberffraw flourished for a time.

Towards the close of the twelfth century, Prince Llywelyn became ruler of the principality of Gwennyd, the successor state to the Roman Empire covering northern Wales. Having sustained a reign of more than 40 years marked by numerous armed conflicts, Llywelyn was subsequently given the name "Great" by Welsh historians.

While in residence at his hunting lodge in Trefiw, Llywelyn was said to have built the Llanrhychwyn church for his wife, Joan, daughter of England's King John. The straight, rectangular lines of the structure and curved wooden beams supporting the ceiling are consistent with architecture of that time.

When we entered the small church on a rainy summer Sunday afternoon, two parishioners were preparing for the service scheduled to begin at 2 pm.

They graciously shared revered centuries-old highlights, such as the square stone baptismal font, aged oak door hung low with wooden hinges, coffin bier hanging on the back wall, and stained glass windows dating back to the fifteenth century. They pointed to one window portraying a somber God peering over Christ on the cross, where upon close examination, God's hand could be seen holding up the cross.

Sensing that Owen had several more storied locales to show us, we knew we couldn't stay for the church service. So we bid farewell to our friendly hosts and pushed onward to a nearby marker, memorializing the sixth century literary figure, Taliesin.

Approaching the site, we passed by Llyn Gerririonydd, which Bernard called a hidden lake, because of its remote nature. Situated high above Trefriw, the lake tranquilly shimmered alongside the forested slopes of Mynydd Deulyn (Mountain of the Two Lakes). Though maintained as part of Gwydyr Forest Park by the Welsh Government, the lake appeared to be a well-kept secret of the local residents.

On the far side of the lake we spotted the Taliesin monument, just up from the shore on a grassy green knoll. As Abel Heywood described in his 1869 **Tourists' Guide to North Wales**, the lake "is renowned as having had on its margin the abode of Taliesin, 'the chief of the bards.' He is said to have been found when a babe on the shores of the lake by

Gwyddno Garanhir in the sixth century." As Heywood reported a century and a half ago, Taliesin was "cherished by the Welsh people" even then. He shared that a prophecy of Taliesin's "relating to the Ancient Britons, is still extant, and has been remarkably verified; it is as follows: - 'Their God they shall worship; their language they shall retain; their land they shall lose, except wild Wales.'"

However, the location for the monument was disputed even back in the nineteenth century. As Joseph Hemingway reported in his 1842 book, **Panorama of the Beauties, Curiosities, and Antiquities of North Wales**, "Lord Willoughby d'Eresby has lately erected a monument which his lordship intended should identify the spot where the poet resided; but unfortunately his lordship has mistaken the site, and placed the column at the west end of the lake, when it is very well known that Taliesin was addressed at Llidiard Coed y Blawd, at the east side of the lake."

For we modern travelers, either end of this enchanting lake could be equally appreciated for the inspiring quality that the revered poet found here. Lori and I had first encountered Taliesin when visiting the Welsh architect Frank Lloyd Wright's winter home, Taliesin West, in far off Arizona. Wright admired the poet and sensed that architecture developed and evolved from folk legend and myth, much like Taliesin's work.

From the hidden lake, we retraced our steps and headed toward a hidden valley south of Betws-y-Coed. On the way however, we stopped at the not so hidden, but still fascinating Tŷ Hyll, the Ugly House. Along the main road between Betws-y-Coed and Capel Curig, the Ugly House appeared as an odd structure whose sides and chimney bulged with misshaped rocks and boulders. Legend has it that a couple of nefarious characters from the fifteenth century invoked an old tradition which stated that if a house was built in a day, the dwelling and surrounding land became the property of the builders. The four foot thick walls, crudely thrown together using moss instead of mortar, gave credence to the incredible story.

Preserved nowadays by the Snowdonia society, the Ugly House has been transformed into an invitingly cozy tea room and visitor center. Taking note of that, Lori and I returned later for a traditional lunch of Welsh rarebit. The Society has transformed the second floor into an informative exhibit of their local honeybee breeding program, established to support the threatened species. As the exhibit points out, the importance of honey goes back thousands of years. In the tenth through twelfth centuries, the Old Laws of Hywel Dda demanded fines for honey theft. Hywel Dda was a Welsh king from the House of Dinefwr, which competed with the House of Aberffraw for dominance in Wales.

Back on the road, we proceeded to remote Cwn Penamnen valley, near the village of Dolwyddelan. Here what remains of Tai Penamnen reminded us of American Indian ruins that are prevalent in the western United States. All that is left of this fifteenth century community are piles of stones outlining the pattern of the original dwellings. At some time in the past, a landslide had swept over the buildings leaving them hidden from sight.

Owen walked us through the archeological excavation site, which early on was the residence of Maredudd ab Ieuan, a later successor to Llewlyn the Great through the House of Aberffraw. Maredudd was also founder of the Wynn family of Gwydir.

Beginning as a single dwelling, Tai Panamnen was expanded over the centuries by a variety of owners, including a poet and musician, Angharad James, until finally being abandoned early in the twentieth century. Owen pointed out a well and bee boles in the remains of the wall. Bee boles were the ancient predecessors of the modern bee hives, such as those described at the Ugly House.

Nearby we spotted the square, three story gray tower of Dolwyddelan Castle, looming from the top of a prominent hill. Guarding a main route, the castle was thought to be built by Llewlyn the Great in the 13th century. Known to have captured a number of castles during his rule, Llewlyn was considered, from a practical standpoint, to be the first Prince of Wales because of the reach of his power, though he never claimed that title. He was instrumental in the effort that forced his father-in-law, King John to sign the Magna Carta in 1215.

Dolwyddelan Castle came into play for the House of Aberffraw again in the 15th century when Maredudd ab Ieuan acquired and upgraded the fading bastion for his residence, prior to moving to Tai Penamnen. In between times, the armies of England's King Edward I had controlled the castle for awhile when Wales was conquered in the late 13th century.

Even Lord Willoughby d'Eresby, mentioned above in connection with Taliesin's monument, had a role restoring Dolwyddelan Castle in the 19th century. As it turns out, Willoughby became owner resulting from his standing as a descendent of the Wynn family of Gwydir.

Squeezing in one final stop before returning to Tan-y-foel, Owen paused the car for a moment by picturesque Pont Fawr, a narrow three-arch stone bridge over the River Conwy in Llanwrst. The bridge was built in 1636 by Sir Richard Wynn, yet another descendent of the House of Aberffraw. Llanwrst, like Trefriw, was known in earlier times for the wool trade. Nowadays, tourism is a bigger draw. The pretty little town afforded a fitting end for our journey, given that the parish church there was the final resting place of Llwylyn the Great.

With our foray to out of the way spots now finished, Lori and I marveled at the rich history that accompanied the seemingly obscure hidden gems that Owen had shared with us. So much so that the next day we returned to another of the lost treasures that we had originally found with Owen. Fairy Glen is an enchanting little gorge accessible by a popular walk from Betws-y-Coed. Owen described a legend that claimed if you went there on the night of a full moon in summer and sat on a rock in the glen, then a fairy would tap you on the shoulder and talk with you.

Fairy Glen, while beautifully scenic, exuded an eerie quality that was spooky enough that we decided against tempting the legend at night. Instead, in the afternoon we located the unique place along the glen that eluded all but the most thoroughgoing visitor. Looking down on Fairy Glen through thick trees and ferns from an old stone bridge crossing the Machno river, another much more ancient bridge could be seen. Dating to the 14th century, now overgrown with hanging greenery, the narrow bridge had served drovers of that era tending their cattle and sheep. We could only imagine if any of the characters from our visit to the other sites had placed foot on this bridge so long ago.

The following morning, our sojourn at Tan-y-foel drew to a close. Over one final sumptuous breakfast, we entertained our hosts, Ria and Chris, with tales of wonder gleaned from the nearby hallowed settings, whose historic events and people we had but glimpsed from afar. Grateful for the information, Ria then asked, "Have you been to the slate mines. They're full of history." "No," I said, "but that gives us an excuse to return someday."

Part 4 – Cornwall and England

Stonehenge

St. Michael's Mount

Chapter 15
Stonehenge

Timeless site evokes Celtic mystery and mystique

Note: A version of this chapter was first published in Celtic Life International, February 2017.

Times had changed in the forty years since my wife, Lori, and I had last viewed Stonehenge firsthand. Back then, a pilgrim could wander in and around the huge stone monoliths, touching and leaning against the cold silent columns, while contemplating the mystery of how they came to be and why.

We were not alone back then, but the number of fellow travelers paled in comparison to the multitudes we found ourselves among on our recent return to this ancient manmade wonder. Rather than complaining though, we were breathing a sigh of relief when we discovered just how close we had come to competing for space with a much greater horde of enthusiasts. Only through some quick, last minute maneuvering were we able to avoid inadvertently arriving at Stonehenge on the day of the summer solstice, when the sun rises directly over the strategically placed

"Heel Stone." While holding profound meaning for the tens of thousands that descend on the monument for that unique experience, for us just the usual crowds on a non-solstice day were challenge enough to contend with.

The routine masses were now kept in check, first by requiring an orderly queue at the relatively new visitor center, followed by a short shuttle bus ride to the actual site. There a safe distance is maintained several yards away from the multi-ton stones, by a rope cordon.

To be fair, the National Trust has done a commendable job in crowd control while providing attractive educational opportunities to learn all about the world heritage site. A highlight of the visitor center is the 360 degree "Stand in the Stones" experience which gives the sense of being within the stone circle, while taking the viewer through a progressive visual chronology of how the site may have looked down through time, as well as during the winter and summer solstice.

Walking outside the visitor center, near the realistic recreation of a Stonehenge era village, we noticed the first direct tie to Celtic lands. Specimens on display of Stonehenge boulders represented the two rock types that formed the monument. The larger Sarsen stones, composed of sandstone and weighing up to 50 tons, originate from the Marlborough Downs area 20 miles away. However, the smaller, four-ton, bluestones, long considered to have originated in the Preseli Hills in Pembrokeshire, Wales, about 150 miles away, have given rise to a recently renewed controversy over their origin and how they got here, freshly stoking an age-old mystery.

Scientists first theorized the Welsh origin of the bluestones about a hundred years ago. Further studies since then have led to general acceptance of that theory. Then in December, 2015, archeologists completing a multiple year dig, claimed to have found the specific quarry at Craig Rhos-y-felin in Pembrokeshire , pinpointing the source of the bluestones. That claim has now been disputed in recent months by another group of scientists, who contend that the quarry-like features at Craig Rhos-y-felin are in fact natural occurrences, with no evidence of man-made intervention. These scientists furthermore renewed another long-contended theory, that glacial action brought the bluestones to the Salisbury Plain, and not the colossal efforts of the early people.

A stone harder than granite, bluestones had also given rise to old folk tales that attributed magical healing qualities to them, perhaps justifying their transport from such a long distance. Even this theory is disputed by those who contend that there was no such use found at Welsh sites, and the stones appear to have arrived at Stonehenge too early in time to even be associated with this idea. Another view, however, poses a connection to an ancestral identity that Welsh settlers wanted to bring with them, possibly joining it with the local tradition.

Whether these or other theories prove true, a walk around the path circling the magnificent monument reinforces the notion that the bluestones must have displayed uniquely special qualities to justify their transport from such great a distance so long ago. Viewing them today, the size and presence of the bluestones pale in comparison to the towering sarsen stones, which at over 20 feet tall stand more than twice as high as the bluestones. Though originally 80 bluestones formed an inner circle and horseshoe within the more prominent sarsen outer circle, many have been removed or broken over the ages, leaving the remaining specimens to appear in a less orderly pattern.

With heads filled with wonder and immense respect for the ancient ones who erected Stonehenge, we retreated to nearby Troutbeck Guesthouse in East Chisenbury for a time of quiet reflection. Sitting on the back deck of our room in the rural setting, we sipped on wine while watching a family of swans leisurely float by on the River Avon, a mere twenty feet away. The Avon also winds its way near Stonehenge, a possible means of transport for the bluestones, as well as for the dead being carried from neighboring prehistoric sites.

The next day we walked around another mysterious stone circle complex, this time in Avebury, about 20 miles north of Stonehenge, in the Marlborough Downs region mentioned above. While not as striking as Stonehenge, the Avebury stone circles are surrounded by a circular earthen berm, a thousand yards in circumference, encompassing a large portion of the village of Avebury. Then an outer stone circle with a thousand foot diameter encloses two inner circles. In total, there were originally thought to be over one hundred stones in the complex. Quarried nearby, the stones range up to forty tons or more in weight and rise ten to eighteen feet high.

A distinct advantage when walking these circles is the freedom to touch and experience the immense stones close up. Other than loosely forming the shape of a circle, the Avebury stones do not appear to display the sophisticated workings or design of Stonehenge.

While strolling the pathway, we encountered two Bobbies on patrol. They were cordial but looked a little out of place. We asked for directions and what they were expecting. "With the coming solstice, the stone circle draws crowds," one replied. "But with the overcast skies and rain threatening, the enthusiasts appear to be holding off."

A little further along, we found a dozen solstice devotees gathered near a standing stone, making ready to celebrate the dawn of summer. One curious group member, seeing us reading from a brochure, approached with a somewhat confused look on his face. "Do you know what this is all about?" he queried.

Unsure of his intent, we offered him our brochure, which he perused. Thanking us, he returned to the group, still appearing oblivious, but resigned to carry on. A friend had most likely talked him into joining the fun without belaboring the details.

Later on, when settled into the aptly named Covenstead B & B in nearby Glastonbury, our hostess, an aficionado of all things occult, explained that the group we met at Avebury was most likely enacting a pagan or druid ritual related to the solstice. A little nervous about the occult-themed nature of our accommodation, we opted that night for the Handfasting Honeymoon Suite, hoping that any untoward spirits would prefer less uplifting rooms. Handfasting was an old Celtic tradition where the newly wed couple's hands were literally bound together, symbolizing their commitment to stay together eternally.

Waking refreshed the next morning and having experienced no strange occurrences during the night, we were treated to a sumptuous breakfast by our hostess, who proceeded to describe another mystery connecting Stonehenge, Glastonbury and Avebury to the Celtic world. The locations of Glastonbury and Avebury put them directly on the St. Michael Ley Line. Furthermore, Stonehenge, through a geometric, geographic correlation, though not situated physically on that Ley Line, has an indirect connection.

Since I had never previously heard of a "ley line," Lori gave me a quick lesson. According to Wikipedia, "Ley lines are apparent alignments of places of significance in the geography or culture of an area, often including man-made structures. They are in the older sense, ancient, straight trackways in the British landscape, or in the newer sense, spiritual and mystical alignments of land forms."

The term originated from British archeologist Alfred Watkins, who in 1921 noticed what appeared to be alignments of ancient monuments and geographical features across Britain. He concluded at the time that they were early trackways, as described in his book, *The Old Straight Track*. Though Watkins drew no spiritual significance to the lines, in recent times such theories have created renewed interest in them.

While there are various theories as to the origins and meaning of ley lines, solid evidence is hard to come by. Some draw a religious purpose, possibly of guides that led ancient ones to sacred places or burial chambers. Others try to connect them with the earth's magnetic field.

The St. Michael Ley Line is considered astronomical, since it follows the route the sun takes on the spring festival of St. Michael, the 8th of May. The geometric theory comes into play with Stonehenge, since the St. Michael Ley Line through Glastonbury and Avebury forms a perfect right triangle with the location of Stonehenge.

Skeptics contend that with the proliferation of ancient monuments and geographic features in the British Isles and greater Europe, ley lines can be conjured up by drawing lines in just about any direction. Irrespective of the veracity of the ley line theories, Stonehenge has been identified as the hub of several ley lines, even a circular one. The relationship to the St. Michael Ley Line provided the second tie-in to the Celtic world that Lori and I noted. Heading in a southwesterly direction after passing through Avebury and Glastonbury, the line proceeds like an arrow across Cornwall all the way to St. Michael's Mount at the tip of the protruding peninsula. That was reason enough for us to explore the picturesque Cornish Celtic countryside enroute to the line's namesake origin.

The next day, navigating our way through Cornwall, we decided on the picture-postcard fishing village of Port Isaac as our base of operations. Port Isaac is on the northern coast of Cornwall, about two-thirds of the way from Glastonbury to St. Michael's Mount. Fans of the British television series, Doc Martin, will recognize the village as Port Wenn, the setting for the medical comedy drama. In fact, our lodging was the old schoolhouse from the show, which has been converted into The Old Schoolhouse Hotel. The dramatic view from our second floor bedroom windows took in the village and seafront to the left, and

Doc Martin's home and surgery directly across the harbor.

Though we could have sat for hours absorbing the idyllic scene from that historic perch, our immediate objective the following day was St. Michael's Mount, a couple hours further south. Nearing the western tip of Cornwall, the road turned toward the southerly coast approaching Mount Bay, near the entrance to the English Channel. To our front, rising majestically 250 feet from the sea, stood the regal form of the St. Michael's Mount castle and chapel, separated from the mainland by a narrow sand causeway, about a half mile in length.

Legend has it that in the fifth century St. Michael the Archangel first touched down on earth at the peak of the isle. We were surprised that this sacred figure was so closely associated with what for some is a rather fantastical, metaphysical concept of the ley line. St. Michael, after all, is known as a condemner of paganism and heresy, and is a patron saint of Cornwall. Nevertheless, the St. Michael Ley Line got its name from the number of religious structures the line passes through, such as churches bearing St. Michael's name on Brent Tor in Brentor, Wales and on Glastonbury Tor.

King Arthur also comes into play along the ley line. He is said to have battled one of the giants that folklore maintains built the isle of St. Michael's Mount. The purported grave of King Arthur and his queen, Guinevere, can be observed today in the midst of the Glastonbury Abbey ruins. He even may have used the route of the ley line as a hunting path.

Fortunate to arrive at St. Michael's Mount during low tide, we gingerly walked the quarter mile cobblestone way from the mainland beach out to the isle. Passing through the village-like setting of shops, gardens and restaurants, we continued up the path to the castle. Along the way, we spotted a small stone heart set amidst the cobblestones. From another legend of giant killers, the heart is all that remains of a vicious giant, Comoran, who terrorized the island inhabitants during King Arthur's time. However, the giant killer this time was a lad named Jack. He dug a pit, then covered it over, so that when Comoran passed, he fell in, with just his head sticking out. Jack slayed him, becoming the hero, Jack the giant killer.

The trek to the castle was steep and the stones uneven, but we finally made it. On this gorgeous sunny day we were captivated by the panoramic view, stretching for miles out to sea and inland, far beyond the bayside resort town of Marazion.

While early history is sketchy, in 1080 CE the Earl of Cornwall, a half-brother of William the Conqueror, granted ownership of St. Michael's Mount to its larger counterpart, the Mont-St-Michel in France. While under French control, the church was completed in the twelfth century. Henry V took back dominion for Britain in 1414. Then in 1659, Colonel John St Aubyn acquired the property, beginning an unbroken tenue of over 350 years, which continues today with the twelfth generation family of James St Aubyn, who still resides in the castle. Though they turned most of the island over to the National Trust in 1954, the St Aubyn's retain a 999 year lease to live in the castle and run the visitor business.

As our time delving into Celtic mysteries was drawing to a close, a final coincidental connection came to our attention. In the year 1275 a powerful earthquake simultaneously destroyed the churches on St, Michael's Mount and Glastonbury Tor. Digging further, we discovered a 2003 book, LEY LINES AND EARTH ENERGIES, *An Extraordinary Journey Into the Earth's Natural Energy System,* by David Cowan and Chris Arnold, that describes a line of earthquake epicenters that coincide with the St. Michael Ley Line.

Though people at the time may not have grasped the possible scientific explanation for the phenomenon, mystical religious connotations were readily and fearfully envisioned. In 1755 on November 1, All Saints Day, a similar, yet even more destructive earthquake struck. Known as the Great Lisbon earthquake, the magnitude 8.5-9 tremor caused such massive devastation, that many feared that the wrath of God had invoked divine judgment.

The diverse scientific, religious and superstitious theories of the Celtic past are certain to perplex visitors and locals alike for a long time to come. Even so, the opportunity to experience these people and places first-hand is sure to enrich the journey.

167

Port Isaac (Port Wenn)

Port Isaac Schoolhouse

Chapter 16
Sweet Dreams at Doc Martin's Schoolhouse
Cornwall's charming Port Isaac

Note: A version of this chapter was first published in Celtic Life International, February 2018.

Shaken from my slumber while dozing in the schoolhouse featured on the popular British comedy-drama series, Doc Martin, I half expected to see Martin's estranged wife, teacher Louisa Ellingham, peering sternly over me as I cleared the cobwebs from my eyes. But no, it was my not-so-estranged wife, Lori, urging me awake to take in the beautifully sunlit Port Isaac harbor from our second floor bedroom window.

The Doc Martin schoolhouse in fictional Port Wenn had been converted to the twelve room Old Schoolhouse Hotel & Restaurant. With rooms named after various school subjects, we were staying in the spacious English bedroom, with glorious views of the Port Isaac village and seafront, which serves as the setting for the long-running TV show.

The Doc Martin series, for which we are avid fans, had given us a glimpse, albeit with a bit of fantasy, of daily life in this idyllic, picturesque fishing village along the northern coast of Cornwall. Even so, spending a few nights here, including frequent extended gazes across the harbor from our unique perch, over to Fern Cottage, the two story brick house used for Doc Martin's surgery, gave the experience a whole new meaning.

Approaching Port Isaac the day before, we kept an eye out for the castle in Tintagel, a few miles to the north. Legend has it that King Arthur was born, or at least conceived, there. Spotting a likely structure high on a prominent bluff overlooking the sea, we parked in town and walked the half mile to the entrance, only to discover that the stately building was not the ancient castle, but the Camelot Castle Hotel. Nonetheless, with the unobstructed 360° views from the hotel looking down over Barras Head, we were able to observe the ancient Tintagel Castle ruins down below.

Winded from the uphill climb to the hotel, we opted for a relaxing afternoon tea in the lounge, while contemplating the far reaching view from the window. The visit proved fortuitous as it turns out, since the hotel itself had been featured in the opening episode of Doc Martin, where the Doc first interviewed for the post as Port Wenn's sole general practitioner.

Fans will recall that Martin had been a successful surgeon in London, but was forced to give that up when he developed a severe fear of blood. Though possessing extraordinary medical acumen, Martin was remarkably lacking in social skills, leading to some heroic, yet painfully hilarious situations. Hence, the first episode was titled *Going Bodmin*, implying a person who is somewhere between wandering adrift and going a bit mad. (Bodmin was a Cornish asylum in the nineteenth century).

The Camelot Castle Hotel appeared several times again, most notably in the fifth season, when Doc Martin's baby son was kidnapped by the quirky pharmacist, Mrs. Tishell, who had a not so secret unrequited romantic obsession for Martin. The Doc and Louisa frantically searched the hotel, disrupting a wedding reception in the process, before discovering that Mrs. Tishell had fled to a different "castle."

Chuckling over these show memories, we looked the hotel over one more time and then proceeded on to Port Isaac and the Old Schoolhouse. I was glad the route brought us in by the backside of the village, since navigating the narrow and congested lane through the tiny seafront center of town appeared doable only for a seasoned villager.

The compact feel of the village took on inescapable immediacy for us anyway, as we drove into the Hotel's minuscule parking lot. Seen as a playground on the TV program, the lot's few densely jammed-in parking spaces were all occupied on this sunny afternoon.

While I contemplated the prospect of the nearest public parking a half mile outside of the village, Lori noticed a small sign on the side of the Hotel: more parking in rear. Our spirits were lifted momentarily.

That is, until we pulled close to the driveway that led to the back. Though our rental car was fairly compact to start with, the clearance on each side, between the Hotel wall and the opposite stone-wall fence, was mere inches. Not much room for error. Nonetheless, I inched along the tight passage, grimacing at the thought of the inevitable scrapes on the car's sides that were sure to come.

Just then, a hotel guest, enjoying a drink on the patio with her companion, observed our plight and jumped up to direct us through the narrows. After an agonizingly slow movement we thought would never end, we finally reached the back unscathed, and were rewarded with several available parking spaces. Not everyone had been so lucky. The car next to ours displayed a freshly incurred gash along its midsection.

Promising the helpful guest a drink, Lori and I proceeded to reception, in dire need of a drink ourselves. A few minutes later, check-in complete and Guinness pint in hand, we retreated to the comfy sofa in the English bedroom, content to absorb the peaceful ambiance of the picture-postcard panorama before us.

Later, refreshed by the serene surroundings, we ventured out on foot to explore the village. As expected, the walk from the school house through the village and up to Fern Cottage took but a few short minutes. The effectiveness of the filming technique achieved in the show was apparent. Before long, a feeling grew within us that we were no longer in Port Isaac, but had stepped into Port Wenn.

That intimacy with the Port Wenn spirit was put in perspective the next day by the contemporary realities of Port Isaac. Eager to experience what living in this captivating village was really like, we joined life-long native, John Brown, for a walking tour.

John and his brother Jeremy come from a long line of local fisherman. Jeremy still goes out fishing for lobster and crab, which are sold in the family business, Just Shellfish, on the waterfront. After the tour, we stopped for some delicious fresh crab sandwiches at The Mote, a friendly restaurant just down the street.

John spent over an hour showing us all the Doc Martin filming locations in the village. Our fantasy was initially broken to learn that Doc Martin's Surgery (Fern Cottage), and Bert Large's restaurant, a large white edifice dramatically perched on a ledge above the beach, were actually vacation homes or rentals. However, the most surprising discovery was that Mrs. Tishell's pharmacy is actually a candy store. A complete make over and rearranging of furnishings transformed the cute little storefront. Show aficionados will enjoy a subtle clue to Mrs. Tishell, even in the real life rendition of the shop. Up on the storefront facade is a wooden ship figurehead of Lord Nelson wearing a neck support. On the show, Mrs. Tishell wears a neck support to protect her Torticollis (twisted neck syndrome).

During the walk, we queried John about the current state of the fishing business. Coincidentally at the time we were there, the British Brexit vote was coming up in a few days. John had plenty to say about that. For his family and fellow fisherman, the European Union had been devastating. The extensive breadth of the English coastline had given fisherman a wealth of fishing rights prior to Britain's joining the EU. Once part of the EU, the rights allocated to England were a small fraction of the original extent. Consequently, much of the fishing industry dried up for the British. Therefore, John and his family were definitely in the "Leave" camp, wanting to return to their past standing.

As we traveled through Britain in the following days, we found much confusion over the vote, and a split in allegiances. Generally, the older generation wanted to leave the EU, preferring the traditional old ways, while the preponderance of the younger generation wished to stay, looking to the expected future benefits. The morning the results were announced, we sensed a shock wave throughout the country, with the unexpected "Leave" side winning. Our bed and breakfast hosts were noticeably distressed and glum.

Upon completing the Port Isaac walking tour and lunch, we spent the afternoon exploring the village's back alleyways and harbor on our own. At the waterfront, Doc Martin had been seen on occasion racing across the sandy beach to administer emergency treatment to a local suffering from some unfortunate mishap. Now, with the tide at its lowest ebb, the few fishing boats that had not gone to sea that day sat high and dry on the exposed seabed. Walking out along the rocky edge, we even came upon a spooky looking sea cave that no doubt was used by smugglers in earlier times.

On our final morning, we lingered over breakfast in the hotel dining room, most likely a converted classroom. The meals here had been delicious, including this day's full Cornish breakfast of eggs, bacon, sausage, mushrooms, stewed tomatoes, toast, and of course, a generous helping of baked beans.

John Brown had mentioned that he actually attended school here when he was a boy. But now, though exterior shots for the TV show are taken here, the interior schoolroom scenes are filmed in a similar, currently active school a few miles away in Delabole. As a matter of fact, interior settings of the Doc's surgery, as well as many others are taped in a converted barn up above the village at Roscarrock Farm, whose manor house coincidentally served as Nampara, the home of Ross Poldark from the Poldark TV series.

We reluctantly bid farewell to Port Isaac and the world of Doc Martin. Back home watching reruns, while anxiously anticipating the new upcoming season of the show, our viewing took on a new meaning. We forevermore felt like we were walking the very streets and backroads of Port Wenn beside the Doc, as he skillfully, and with a scowl on his face, served his lovable, accident-prone, villagers.

Adelphi Theatre London

Regent Theatre Melbourne

Chapter 17

Tale of Two Phantoms

How globalization saved Love Never Dies

"It was the best of times. It was the worst of times." Stepping onto the stage to a rousing standing ovation at the Regent theatre in Melbourne one September, Andrew Lloyd-Webber must have had similar feelings to those expressed in Charles Dickens' *Tale of Two Cities*.

Only a month earlier, *Love Never Dies,* his long awaited sequel to *Phantom of the Opera,* had closed in London after a disappointing eighteen month run. Some may say that a show playing in London or Broadway for a full year and a half must at least be OK. But this was an Andrew Lloyd-Webber show, the successor to *Phantom of the Opera*, which not only holds the record for longest running musical on Broadway, but one that can still be seen there today after more than twenty-five years.

While *Tale of Two Cities* portrays the socially repressive parallels between eighteenth century London and Paris, comparisons between London and Melbourne also extend back to that period. The British dealt with deprivation by transporting convicts to Australia, though mainly to places other than Melbourne, which came into its own with the discovery of gold in the same mid-nineteenth century decade that Dickens' novel was published.

But for a twenty-first century Lloyd-Webber, it was the vast distance between London and Melbourne, and a creative new production team, that provided the space and fresh approach needed to re-launch his sequel far from the bad press of the initial incarnation.

During the original London production, my wife, Lori, and I had arrived at the Savoy Hotel, just down the street from the Adelphi Theatre, where *Love Never Dies* had opened seven months earlier. At the end of our vacation, we eagerly anticipated seeing the show and then relaxing before returning home to the States in two days. But first a different surprise awaited us.

The Savoy first opened in 1889, a century after Dickens' Madame Defarge and other revolutionaries stormed the Bastille in Paris. However, until three weeks before our arrival, the most famous of London's grand hotels, had been closed for three years, when an expected seventeen month, $150 million renovation mushroomed to more than $300 million. Even so, we had no idea what was in store as the shadows lengthened on that autumn Tuesday.

The doorman directed us to a member of the hotel staff, who led us through the gleaming Front Hall, rich with wood panels, elegant Edwardian furnishings and fixtures, all vibrant with the look and feel of a new palace. We passed numerous hotel staff, all spit and polished, milling around a bit anxiously, as well as a large contingent of guests decked out in black tie. A cute little gray speckled dog was leading a man around by his leash, sniffing away as if on a mission. We started to feel out of place in our tennis shoes and casual travel clothes, having just arrived from Heathrow Airport.

Happy to be led off to the quieter Reading Room, a welcome alternative to a registration counter, we were seated at one of several desks, and at last could ask some of the pressing questions that were forming in our minds. "What's happening here?" I queried. "Tonight's the Grand Reopening Champagne Reception," the staff member beamed. "The Prince is expected to arrive between 6:30 and 7." My quizzical gaze peered cluelessly, as if to ask "the Prince?" Sensing my confusion, he added, "Prince Charles is coming."

Now things were beginning to make sense: the nervous staff, the classy guests, and the apparent bomb-sniffing dog. "What should we do, stay out of the way?" I asked incredulously. The amused response was that, as hotel residents, we were welcome to partake in the festivities, have some champagne and canapés. That part sounded enticing, since the day's travel connections caused us to miss lunch.

Even more enticing was the suite on the seventh floor that we were given as a complimentary upgrade. Like all other areas of the hotel, the suite was sparkling and new. Edwardian styles decorated the bedroom and sitting room, which were joined by a foyer with marble bathroom in between. From the windows, boats could be seen plying the river Thames, as city lights offset the fading daylight.

By 5:30 we were on our way down the elevator. The Front Hall was abuzz with excitement, with guests conversing intensely, and staff hurriedly polishing lamps and furniture one more time. On one side, the news media was interviewing Princess Amira, wife of Prince Alwaleed of Saudi Arabia, one of the Hotel's owners. We found a strategic spot next to the stairway leading down to the Thames foyer. Word had it that the Prince of Wales would be led this way on his tour.

Shortly after six, Prince Alwaleed, his entourage and the Hotel staff proceeded out the front door followed by the guests, to greet Prince Charles when he appeared. Before long, a myriad of photo flashes confirmed to us that His Royal Highness had indeed arrived. Greeting formalities and respects were exchanged as the Prince made his way, talking with various dignitaries and staff as he went.

After a few minutes, guests and media rushed back inside, followed by Prince Charles and Prince Alwaleed, escorted by Savoy General Manager, Kieran MacDonald. Our cameras were at the ready as they approached. Animated in discussion, Prince Charles glanced our way as he passed. Seeing us, he struck a pleasant pose, smiling for the cameras, before proceeding on to the Thames Foyer, stopping on the way at Savoy Tea, a new shop where pastries and candies are handmade, using Valrhona chocolate imported from France.

Upon completion of the tour, Prince Charles returned to the Front Hall, conversing with guests while hotel staff scurried around, assuring that champagne glasses were kept full. The two princes then unveiled a marble plaque and addressed the assembled group. They were both pleased with the restoration that had returned the Savoy to the elegance of its past. Prince Charles enjoyed seeing that long term Savoy employees had returned to carry on the tradition. He remarked that his grandmother loved the Savoy and would have approved of the workmanship and beautiful results attained.

Prince Charles completed his speech and then bid farewell just after 7 pm. But we had no time to savor what had just taken place. There was a 7:30 curtain time for *Love Never Dies*. Fortunately, the Adelphi Theatre was just a block away. We rushed up the elevator, which had been stopped during the Prince's visit, grabbed our coats, and were off to the show.

Settled in our orchestra seats a few minutes later, we watched the story unfold with the Phantom reappearing in New York's Coney Island of 1907, ten years after his mysterious disappearance from the depths of the Paris opera House. Though Lloyd-Webber first thought of doing a sequel early in the 1990's, he took his time wanting to find just the right narrative before proceeding. Once there, he used his technique of private workshops to get the storyline and staging just right. Or so he thought.

When *Love Never Dies* premiered in March 2010, the critics were generally unimpressed. The music was classic Lloyd-Webber and the sets engaging enough, but the plot was left wanting. At least that's what the Scrooge-like critics felt.

As Lori and I departed the theatre, copies of a letter from The Lord Lloyd-Webber himself were being handed to all theatergoers. "I hope you have enjoyed today's performance. I am very proud of "Love Never Dies" but I am a restless, perfectionist soul. There is still a lot of work I want to do on the show so we are going to close it for a few days in November and re-open it on Friday November 26th." He went on to offer discounted tickets for the reworked show when it returned. "There is just one catch – you must please give real feedback…"

Alas, our stay in London was at an end, so we would have to be satisfied reading the updated reviews for the new version. While some of those reviews turned out to be better, the return of the Phantom was still considered a disappointment, and the musical closed in August.

To be fair, during the final months of preparation for the opening, Lloyd-Webber was diagnosed with prostate cancer, leaving him distracted and incapacitated during the critical period where he would normally have a close eye on the smallest detail that can turn a show into a success.

Lloyd-Webber is known for his staying power over several decades. So when a dynamic Australian production team offered to give *Love Never Dies* a whole new look, Lloyd-Webber placed his beloved, but flawed work in their hands for a second try. The results were dramatic. A show that some in London had derisively renamed as *Paint Never Dries,* took a magical turn into a huge success at the Regent Theatre in Melbourne.

By lucky happenstance, Lori and I found ourselves in Melbourne that October for business and another vacation. As we arrived downtown, the modern façade of the Crown Promenade Hotel stood out for us in stark contrast to London's Savoy. The hotel is one of three that ring the Crown Entertainment Complex located on the bank of the Yarra River in Melbourne's lively Southbank district, a successful urban renewal project of the past two decades. Complete with a large casino, the experience here was akin to the glitz and glamour more typically associated with Las Vegas.

A guided boat tour on the river offered a pleasant counterpoint to the intensity of the casino. The boat floated along calm waters past the striking skyline, contemporary Federation Square, Picasso-esque Deborah Halpern sculptures, and other highlights like the Rod Laver Arena with the massive Melbourne Cricket Ground (MCG) looming behind it. Australia's largest stadium, the MCG, as locals call it, is remembered for the 1956 Olympics, as well as for serving as a World War II rest and recuperation center for American soldiers fighting in the South Pacific.

Walking back along the river, we stopped to explore the Immigration Museum. There multimedia exhibits chronicle the lives of the nine million immigrants who have come to Australia starting in 1788. The deprivation and hardships of the early days were reminiscent of Dickens' portrayals of that time in Europe.

Suitably relaxed from our river sojourn and a quiet dinner at the hotel, we stepped into the complimentary shuttle van for the short ride to the Regent Theatre. Retaining its traditional European flair, Melbourne's downtown is interlaced with historic and modern trams. Our calm state was suddenly displaced by a shocking feeling of dread when the van driver abruptly cut directly across several lanes of traffic to make a turn. That was our introduction to a unique roadway feature known as the "hook turn." To accommodate the trams proceeding on tracks in the center of the road, vehicles that normally would turn from the center of the road must instead make the turn from the far lane, hopefully waiting until the coast is clear. Assuring us that the maneuver was perfectly normal, our driver continued the journey, bringing us to the theatre without further incident.

We quickly found our seats and took a deep breath with eager anticipation, hoping that our faith in the artistry of Andrew Lloyd-Webber would be restored by what we were about to experience. And then the curtain rose.

Right from the start, we were struck by the lavish staging, brightly colored costumes and effects that brought the carnival atmosphere of turn-of-the-century Coney Island to life. Some reworking of plot and song placement gave more immediacy and coherence to the story. Even though, like many died-in-the-wool Phantom fans, we may have taken the story ultimately in a different direction, we were still dazzled by the richness of this new production. This was indeed the setting that was up to the task of showcasing the mastery of Lloyd-Webber musicality.

At intermission, a lady selling *Love Never Dies* souvenirs told us excitedly that a film producer had recently taped the show for future release. Leave it to Lloyd-Webber to try new, innovative methods to show the world how he wants them to know *Love Never Dies*.

Months later back home, we found ourselves sitting in a cinema, awaiting the screening of the filmed version of the Melbourne production. In an introductory piece, Lloyd-Webber, along with the actors and production team, took the audience through the progression of the Melbourne show, from Australian director Simon Phillips' inspired vision to the triumphant opening night.

Lloyd-Webber described showing a filmed trailer of the play to a friend, who was so taken with the visual imagery that he convinced the creator to bring the complete musical to the big screen. Lloyd-Webber sounded so pleased with this third rendition of the show, that he was likely hoping that the broad release of the film would dispel negative vibrations from the London production, while at the same time advancing the whole art of filmed theatrical productions to a new level. If winning Australia's prestigious Helpman awards for scenic design, costume design and lighting were any indication, that may just happen. The "best of times" had indeed replaced the "worst of times" for Lloyd-Webber.

Watching *Love Never Dies* in the movie theatre, we felt like we were on stage right next to the larger than life performers. The expressions of passion and pain on the faces of the actors projected more powerfully at close range, while Lloyd Webber's richly melodic chords surrounded and permeated the audience. There was plenty of drama as Christine Daae, the now famous soprano, played by the gifted Anna O'Byrne, came to New York to sing opera, bringing along her drunken gambler husband, Raoul, the effectively brooding Simon Gleeson, and ten year old son, Gustave, a youthfully precocious Jack Lyall.

On Coney Island, she once again encountered the Phantom, now a successful side show promoter, that Ben Lewis portrayed with a powerfully tragic persona. Madame Giry (Maria Mercedes) and daughter Meg (Sharon Millerchip) helped the Phantom escape from Paris, and were now in his employ. A renewed struggle for Christine's love ensued between Raoul and the Phantom, building to a surprising climax, stoked by Christine's fervent rendition of the show's towering title song. The acting and vocals of the cast played well, especially with the proximity of the cameras, but the star was by far Lloyd-Webber's emotive score as it soared bountifully and interweaved fluidly among the intense colors and sensations of this bittersweet tale of love and loss.

I initially questioned why Lloyd-Webber would bring to film a production that had not yet appeared on Broadway. Wouldn't that diminish the potential of a successful run? Having now seen both stage and screen, I can tell that they each stand on their own. From the audience of the stage musical, which takes in the broad expanse of the set in one view, the eyes are tantalized by the countless clever details that Lloyd-Webber has incorporated, while the ears are treated to the delicate resonance of the live orchestra. At a film screening, the detail of facial expressions and variety of camera positions closing in and pulling back provides a new whole dimension for viewing a musical.

If you missed the London, Melbourne and film screenings, all is not lost. The DVD provides yet another medium for enjoying the magic of *Love Never Dies*. The timing of the release, in 2012, was fitting, as it was the 200th birthday of Charles Dickens, whose works have flourished on television, theatre and the silver screen.

Part 5
Africa and North America - Celtic World Echoes

Cape of Good Hope

Table Mountain from Mount Nelson Hotel

Chapter 18
Wales at the Southern Tip of Africa?
Celtic culture in the most unlikely of places

Note: A version of this chapter was first published in Celtic Life International, June 2018.

On a recent business trip to Cape Town, South Africa, the name of a picturesque coastal suburb caught my eye, as I passed by enroute to the nearby Cape of Good Hope. Now it is rare that I remember names of big city suburbs on my travels. But for a lover of all things Celtic, this one was hard to miss: Llandudno.

To the Welsh, Llandudno is the name of the beautiful seaside city on the northern coast of Wales, named after the sixth century patron saint, Saint Tudno. Tudno was known to have founded the first church in the Llandudno area. But what has that to do with far off South Africa?

Immediately, my mind started to conjure up the prospects of a hearty group of Welsh pioneers braving a long, arduous sea voyage hundreds of years ago to settle here. Returning home, I dove into South African history with expectant excitement at what might turn up.

Sadly, my colorful fantasies were dashed. The real story was only too mundane. As it turns out, a South

African vacationer to Wales in 1903 was struck by the similar look of the beautiful shoreline at Llandudno, to that of her homeland locale. Upon returning to South Africa, she saw to it that her newly incorporated township was given the same name.

A strictly residential community of upscale homes, South Africa's Llandudno does not even have a shopping center. Indeed, its most famous feature is a secluded nude beach, nestled among granite boulders off a short sandy trail from the side of the town.

Disappointed, but with my interest piqued, I delved further to determine what real Celtic history might emerge from this distant land. I knew of the British impact on South Africa, as so vividly portrayed by my favorite author, James Michener's monumental work, **The Covenant**. The British became influential at the beginning of the nineteenth century, replacing the Dutch who had settled there a couple centuries earlier.

One well-known missionary of this era, David Livingstone, was a Scotsman. Though better known for his explorations further north, he got his start in South Africa, arriving in Cape Town in 1841. He would later write a book of his early time there, titled *Missionary Travels and Researches in South Africa.*

Of special pertinence to the current discussion of the Welsh, some may be surprised to learn of a connection when Livingstone was thought to have been lost in deepest Africa. In the late 1860's, while searching for the source of the Nile River, he had not been heard from in a long time. American journalist, Henry Stanley, a native Welshman, born and raised in Wales before immigrating to the United States at the age of 18, was commissioned in 1869 to locate Livingstone. When he finally found the renowned missionary in 1871 in what is now Tanzania, he purportedly uttered the famous words, "Dr. Livingstone, I presume?" Stanley was also known for explorations and mapping of sections of Africa, as well as for some controversy surrounding his service to Belgian King Leopold in the Congo, where his harsh treatment of Africans was questioned.

Welsh missionaries were also known to be assigned to South Africa in the mid-1800's. Thomas Philipps, son of a clergyman from Pembrokeshire, led an early Welsh party to South Africa in 1820. Philipps had been a partner in the Milford and Pembrokeshire Bank which failed in 1810. Subsequently, when the British Government passed the Cape Emigration Scheme in 1819 to encourage emigration to South Africa, Philipps started a new life, leading a group sailing on the Kennersley Castle. They settled in a place he named Lampeter after the family's home in Wales.

Later, the storied Royal Welsh Fusiliers, one of the oldest infantry units of the British Army, saw commendable service in the south of Africa during the Second Boer War from 1899 to 1902. They fought alongside the Royal Scots Fusiliers and the Royal Irish Fusiliers, together forming the 6th Brigade. The Royal Welsh Fusiliers had a colorful history with action in many conflicts, including the Battle of the Boyne, the American Revolution and the Battle of Waterloo, to name but a few.

The leaders of the British Army's 6th Brigade, Field Marshals Roberts and Kitchener, and General Buller, used the Mount Nelson Hotel in Cape Town as a headquarters. Roberts was Irish and Scotch, while Kitchener was born in Ireland, and Buller was of Cornish descent.

The Mount Nelson, the stately grande dame of Cape Town, is serenely situated in the shadow of Table Mountain which inspired its name, along with that of British naval hero, Lord Nelson. Privileged to stay at the Mount Nelson during my business meetings, I soaked up the colonial elegance that still characterizes this iconic structure, whose rosy-pink aura gave rise to its own unique shade of paint, the "Mount Nelson's Blush."

Welsh miners have been emigrating from Wales to many parts of the world for centuries looking for a better life. As a destination, mineral rich South Africa was no exception. During the mid-nineteenth century, the discovery of gold there brought even more miners hoping to find riches.

Diamonds are the mineral for which South Africa is best known. A Welshman gained fame for discovering the largest rough cut diamond ever found. In 1905, at the Premier mine, Welsh miner Thomas Evan Powell unearthed the 3,106 caret Cullinan diamond and turned it over to his mine superintendent, Frederick Wells. The value of the many diamonds cut from the Cullinan are considered to be worth two billion dollars today. Many of them are found among the British crown jewels.

One of the most lasting Welsh influences in South Africa relates to the country's national anthem. In 1897, a hymn, Nkosi Sikelel' iAfrika, was composed in the Xhosan language by Enoch Sontonga, a Xhosan Methodist missionary. In English, the title translates as *God Bless Africa*. Sontonga set the hymn lyrics to Welshman Joseph Perry's treasured Welsh hymn tune, *Aberystswyth*, which was also immortalized in the well known Charles Wesley composition, Jesus, Lover of my Soul.

Nkosi Sikelel' iAfrika became the national anthem of the African National Congress during Apartheid. Then in 1994, after Apartheid was ended, Nkosi Sikelel' iAfrika was named co-National Anthem of South Africa, along with Die Stem van SuidAfrika, the prior Afrikaans National Anthem, which in English is *The Call of South Africa*. Finally, in 1997, parts from the two anthems were combined to form the current National Anthem of South Africa.

The lyrics of Nkosi Sikelel' iAfrika are:

Lord, bless Africa
May her horn rise high up
Hear Thou our prayers
And bless us.
Chorus
Descend, O Spirit
Descend, O Holy Spirit

Speaking of music, the Welsh Male Voice Choir of South Africa continues the tradition of the Welsh presence in the country. Formed in 1978, the group of more than 40 members performs dozens of concerts a year, in a variety of European as well as African languages. Celebrating their 40 years in 2018, the choir performed a St. David's day concert in Johannesburg on March 3, 2018.

These are just a few highlights of how the Welsh have made their mark on South Africa over recent centuries. Pretty impressive after all. My thanks to picturesque, yet unpretentious Llandudno, South Africa, for sending me on a journey that produced this treasure trove of fascinating, historical encounters. For those wanting to learn more about South Africa, an Englishman aptly named Frank Welsh has written a comprehensive volume, titled *A History of South Africa.*

High Cross by Iona Abbey

Dale Bruner and Gerald Herter

Chapter 19
Connecting With Celtic Spirituality
Through Stillness, Silence and Solitude

Note: A version of this chapter was first published in Celtic Life International, February 2019.

Be still and know that I am God!
-        Psalm 46:10

A year ago, my friend, Carl Greenwood, and I made the trek one Sunday morning from our Orange County, California homes, up to Hollywood Presbyterian Church in nearby Los Angeles. We were going to meet Christian author and scholar Dr. Dale Bruner for brunch. Dr. Bruner had agreed to lead the annual retreat that year for the men at our Tustin Presbyterian Church. So we were meeting to discuss the topic.

Dr. Bruner suggested that we come early and attend the class at Hollywood Presbyterian that was led by his son, Dr. Michael Bruner, professor at Azusa Pacific University.

Of all the many church classes I have taken over the years, few stand out in my memory as this one did. Dr. Bruner was teaching a series and the topic that day was meditation. Effective meditation was the result of three elements: **stillness, silence and solitude**.

As Dr. Bruner was preparing the lesson, a Beatles classic, *The Fool on the Hill*, came to mind, and he found it remarkable that the words from the song hit precisely at what the lesson on meditation was trying to impart.

The song tells about a man sitting quietly by himself without speaking to anyone. In other words, he is still, silent, and in a state of solitude. However, though he is perceived as being inane, in reality he is aware of the truly important things that others miss because of the distractions that they let fill their lives.

Now every time this song comes to mind, I am reminded of that class, and the need to take time to seek God's spirit through the meditative practice of silence, stillness and solitude.

We live in such a busy world, with countless diversions, that it can be hard to find a quiet time to be still and let God speak to us.

A number of years ago, I was introduced to Celtic Spirituality by Dr. Rebecca Prichard, currently a New Theological Seminary of the West professor. At that time, Rebecca was pastor at Tustin Presbyterian Church. Rebecca invited Dr. John Phillip Newell to give a lecture at the church on Celtic Spirituality. Dr.

Newell had been warden at the abbey on the Isle of Iona in Scotland, known as the birthplace of Celtic Spirituality. Rebecca asked my wife, Loretta, and I to host Dr. Newell for the night at our home.

I was up early the next morning to prepare a simple breakfast for Dr. Newell and myself. As we ate, Dr. Newell commented on how he appreciated the peaceful setting, with the view of the hills and valley out our window. His practice was to arise early in the morning for a time of quiet reflection and devotional.

Dr. Newell left with us a copy of his book, **Listening for the Heartbeat of God**. The title is taken from the scene at the last supper, as described in John 13:23 - *Now there was leaning on Jesus' bosom one of his disciples, whom Jesus loved.* One can visualize the disciple John listening at Jesus' chest. We are encouraged to seek God's presence, God's heartbeat, everywhere.

I used to be puzzled by this depiction, since when looking at the painting of the Last Supper, John is leaning away from Jesus. When I was in Milan recently, and privileged to see Leonardo da Vinci's masterpiece, this fact was confirmed. However, a guide pointed out that the painting was just a single moment in time, and just not the same exact moment that is referred to in the scripture.

I am part of a men's breakfast group that has been meeting on Friday mornings since 1980. Recently we studied one of Newell's newer books, **The Rebirthing of God: Christianity's Struggle for New Beginnings**. I think a better title would be, The Rebirthing of God _in Us_, since God does not need rebirthing. We do.

Using different objects from Iona as symbols for each chapter, Newell discusses various aspects of reconnecting. One of those is reconnecting with spiritual practice. Newell uses the remotely located Hermit's Cell on Iona as the symbol. Here St. Columba would come in the 6th century to meditate. Newell also mentions other forms of spiritual practice, such as walking a labyrinth and yoga.

When I entered semi-retirement, Loretta convinced me to take a yoga class with her on Tuesday and Thursday mornings. Along with various positions and exercises, there are moments at the middle and end where there is quiet time when the mind is cleared for sole, silent, still contemplation. While these are perfect occasions to let the Spirit come in, I have to admit that I often find myself taking those moments to plan the rest of my day. Having a type "A," left brain, task-oriented persona, I still have a long way to go to fully reach a complete meditative state in those sessions.

Dr. Newell points out that the term, yoga, is derived from the Sanskrit, meaning a desire to be yoked with the sacred. At the end of each yoga class, we stretch out our arms, and bow our heads to each other as we say, "My soul bows to your soul, Namaste." Namaste actually means "the divine in me bows to the divine in you."

Dr. Newall also refers to Thomas Merton, the Trappist monk, who followed a discipline of silence. For Merton, "spiritual practice is not seeking "to know about God, but to know God...seeking the experience of presence." Or as Carl Jung put it: "I don't need to believe. I know."

Merton used a threefold pattern for spiritual practice: 1) remembering our diamond essence, 2) remembering the diamond essence in everyone and everything, and 3) accessing the diamond essence of our being in order to be strong for the work of transformation in the world. For Merton, the diamond essence referred to the image of God.

Celtic spirituality focuses more on experiencing God in our lives as opposed to ascribing to a set of doctrines. As Dr. Newell puts it:

"Western Christianity…had confused faith with a set of propositional truths about the Divine, rather than a personal experience of the Divine that could be undergirded and sustained by particular practices and disciplines."

This perspective has helped me overcome decades of guilt over the rigid, literal beliefs of the Fundamentalist church I attended during my high school years.

The Celtic approach is also evident in the book, **Rethinking our Story**, *Can We Still be Christian in a Quantum Era?* by Doug Hammock, pastor of North Raleigh Community Church in North Carolina. The author affirms that "Celtic Christians honored diverse ways of experiencing God...Celts focused on divine image breathed into us at creation...By integrating meditative technique with our approach to scripture, we become more discerning...Christian tradition offers a spirituality deeper than learning, deeper than doctrine."

If only in my high school years I had a pastor, like the Rev. Dr. Gary Demarest, renowned Presbyterian minister and church leader. He was honest enough to say, when giving a seminary board meeting devotional a few months ago, something like, "I believe in Jesus and the resurrection, but after all these years I still can't answer the question: What if when I die, it all just turns black?"

We can have faith amid our doubts. As theologian Paul Tillich once said, "Sometimes I think it is my mission to bring faith to the faithless, and doubt to the faithful."

As a final example, I would like to share from the Preface to my new book, **From Ledgers to Ledges**, *Four Decades of Teambuilding Adventures in America's West.* I am a big fan of John Muir. Muir and I have some things in common: like Muir, I am part Scottish, love the outdoors, am Presbyterian, went to the University of Wisconsin, headed west, hiked parts of the Muir Trail, and am a member of the Sierra Club, co-founded by Muir. Nevertheless, I could not hold a candle to all that Muir did for the American West.

Muir was hiking one time in Alaska with Stephen Young, a missionary to the native Indians, who wrote a book about the experience titled **Alaska Days with John Muir**. They were camped at the base of a mountain in Glacier Bay.

As recalled by Young after a rainy night, Muir's gaze upon a mountain brought this breathless exclamation: "'God Almighty!' he said. Following his gaze…I saw the summit highest of all crowned with glory indeed…As we looked in ecstatic silence we saw the light creep down the mountain…Our minds cleared with the landscape…But there was no profanity in Muir's exclamation, 'We have met with God.' A lifelong devoutness of gratitude filled us, to think that we were guided into this most wonderful room of

God's great gallery… 'We saw it! We saw it. He sent us to his most glorious exhibition. Praise God from whom all blessings flow.'"

Halifax Guide by Titanic Victim's Grave

Peggy's Cove Harbor

Chapter 20
A Halifax Tradition of Gratitude and Hope
Caring humans build bridges over differences

Note: A version of this chapter was first published in Celtic Life International, December 2015.

Gazing in the direction of Boston Common from the lofty window of my waterfront hotel room, I was not yet aware of the profound annual tradition that would take place there in the upcoming holiday season. For now my thoughts were filled with expectations of rugged coastlands and changing fall colors. The next day would begin a cruise up the coast of New England, around Nova Scotia and Prince Edward Island, then into the Saint Lawrence Seaway to Quebec, before finishing at Montreal.

Two days later, as my ship cruised into the harbor at Halifax, Nova Scotia, the skyline and active shipping channels gave evidence to the robust commercial center that Halifax had become since the city's formal establishment by the British in 1749. Even so, I was soon to learn of several fatefully poignant events over the past century that revealed the truly resilient and compassionate spirit of the people of Halifax.

On April 15, 1912, the RMS Titanic hit an iceberg and sank, some 700 nautical miles off the coast of Halifax. The 706 survivors were taken to New York. However, four Canadian ships recovered the remains of over 300 bodies from the sea. From those remains, 209 bodies were capable of being saved and were brought to Halifax. Though St. John, Newfoundland was closer, Halifax was better equipped to handle the bodies.

Our Halifax guide, Mel Gosse, took us to Fairview Lawn Cemetery, where most of the Titanic victims were buried. As we walked the four rows of graves, Mel pointed out how the last row bends like the bow of the ship. He also noted a space between graves that appeared to represent where the iceberg had struck. Most of the gravestones were of plain concrete, while a few had been enhanced by relatives. A Celtic cross adorned a tomb of an unknown child. While many graves had names attached, a number were still unidentified.

Members of our group were silent, in somber reflection of the Titanic victims, as we boarded our tour bus. However, as we traveled amidst the grandeur of the terrain and brilliant autumn foliage enroute to the scenic shores of outlying Peggy's Cove, Mel filled the hour with the story of another tragedy much more horrific for the residents of Halifax. Such was the impact that their response is still felt and honored some one hundred years hence.

The morning of December 6, 1917 in Halifax harbor began quietly, but soon became the sight of a terrible disaster. Two ships were speeding through a section called the Narrows, racing to make up time caused by delays the night before.

Because of the danger posed by German U-boats during the ongoing World War I, anti-submarine nets had been employed to close the harbor entrance for the night. The fueling of a Norwegian ship, the SS Imo, bound for New York to pick up relief supplies intended for Europe, took longer than planned, requiring the wait until morning. A French cargo ship, the SS Mont-Blanc, fully laden with TNT and other highly explosive material, also bound for Europe, had planned to join a convoy crossing the Atlantic, but was likewise too late to depart before the harbor closed.

As the harbor reopened in the morning, both ships were moving far above the speed limit and out of their prescribed positions, in hopes of making up for lost time. Approaching each other from opposite directions, they both realized too late that they were on a collision course. Though the impact at 8:45 am did not seriously damage the Mont Blanc, barrels of benzol, a form of benzene, toppled, spilling on the deck, and then igniting from engine sparks as the fluid flowed into the hold.

The huge, ensuing flames intrigued Halifax citizens as they watched from the shore, oblivious of the impending danger. Then at 9:04 am, the TNT exploded in spectacular fashion, in what was the largest man-made explosion prior to the atom bomb. Ship fragments landed as far as three miles away, while a smoke plume rose to almost 12,000 feet above the destroyed harbor. Nearly 2,000 people were killed, while 9,000 suffered injuries. Many were blinded from the glass of blast-shattered windows where they were watching. Many homes were lost as well.

This is where the city of Boston comes in. There was an outpouring of compassion and assistance from many nearby towns, provinces and states. None was more remarkable than the efforts of the Boston community, especially the Boston Red Cross and the Massachusetts Public Safety Committee. When news reached Boston the day of the blast, a train with medical personnel, supplies, food and water was quickly arranged and sent to aid the stricken city and her suffering citizens.

As our guide Mel told the story, the people of Halifax were so touched by the caring outreach from the people of Boston, that the following December 1918, they found the biggest and best Christmas tree in all of Nova Scotia and sent it to Boston as an expression of gratitude. The tradition was revived in 1971, so that each year since, a similar Christmas tree is sent and erected on the Boston Common as a remembrance of the goodwill and kindness of the human spirit. Publisher Angus (Marcie) Macquarrie refers to this remarkable custom in the opening of the tradition-filled December 2017 Christmas issue of Celtic Life International magazine.

As we pondered the depth of traumatic tragedy and response arising from these two events early in the twentieth century, our bus pulled into Peggy's Cove for a welcome respite. Located on the shore of St. Margarets Bay, about 25 miles southwest of Halifax, Peggy's Cove is a rustic fishing village whose ruggedly beautiful setting has captured the hearts of locals and tourists alike. Perched dramatically atop a large glacially carved outcropping of granite, Peggy's Point Lighthouse warns approaching ships of the treacherous coastline.

Walking the uneven rock surface amid the brisk ocean breeze and bright sunlight served to refresh our spirits. Even so, Peggy's Cove played its own part reacting to a time of calamity when SwissAir Flight 111 crashed into the bay on September 2, 1988 killing all 229 aboard. The village provided staging areas to support the search and rescue effort.

On the ride back to Halifax, Mel shared a more recent event, no less filled with incalculable tragedy than the earlier stories. But this one offered the people of Halifax the opportunity to open their arms and hearts to a vast and sudden influx of distressed visitors on September 11, 2001.

When the World Trade Center towers in New York were attacked by terrorists and destroyed, all air traffic into the United States was immediately shut down. Incoming flights had no choice but to abort their flight plans and find the nearest landing field outside the U.S. to put down.

In quick response, the Canadian government initiated Operation Yellow Ribbon, enabling 255 aircraft to divert to 17 different airports across Canada. The most well-known effort was at Gander, Newfoundland, where 38 planes and some 6,600 passengers landed. The humanitarian work of the people there was immortalized in a Broadway musical, *Come From Away*. The show is featured in an October 2017 Celtic Life International article by Managing Editor Stephen Clare, as well as in the February 2019 issue.

Lesser known, but equally heroic was the outreach of the citizens of Halifax on that fateful day. Forty aircraft and some 8,000 passengers found themselves stranded at Halifax's Stanfield International Airport. From personal experience, Mel described the predicament. Sports facilities were immediately opened to accommodate the frightened and confused passengers. However, the arenas and gymnasiums were only able to hold about 2,000 of the unexpected guests, and soon filled up.

An appeal went out, and in no time, many of the local populace stepped forward. Mel and his wife even picked up a family and brought them home. This spontaneous act of kindness was repeated over and over by others in the area until all 8,000, including those initially at the arenas, were welcomed into homes of the people of Halifax. For the next several days, the warmth and empathy of these generous and caring Canadians poured out upon their grateful guests.

The spirit of the 1917 Halifax disaster victims had surely been passed down to their descendants, who were only overjoyed to reach out a helping hand to others found in unplanned and untenable circumstances.

With our day in Halifax drawing to a close as the bus returned us to our ship, we had a new found admiration for this historic city and her gracious and resilient inhabitants.

Taliesin West

Petroglyph with Symbol at Taliesin West

Chapter 21

Frank Lloyd Wright's Taliesin West

A Welsh myth takes hold in the land of the Phoenix

Celtic lore is not what normally comes to mind when one's thoughts turn to Arizona. Ancient mythology in the southwestern United States stems mainly from the Anasazi ancestors of Native American Indian tribes. However, just a short drive north of Phoenix sits a desert complex known as Taliesin West, a very Welsh-sounding name.

In fact, Taliesin West was the western home of world renowned Welsh architect Frank Lloyd Wright. Wright built a home `and architectural school there to escape the harsh winters at his Wisconsin residence.

Wright's mother, Anna Lloyd Jones, emigrated with her family in the mid-nineteenth century from the small town of Llandysul, Wales, in the western county now known as Ceredigion. Though Wright was born near Spring Green, Wisconsin, where his family settled, Welsh lore and myth were an influential part of his heritage.

One such ancient legend began with Cerridwen, a Welsh goddess of dark powers, who was the keeper of a magical cauldron. After boiling for a year and a day, the first three drops of the cauldron's liquid would impart wisdom and inspiration on the recipient, whilst the rest of the molten brew then became poisonous. Cerridwen planned to compensate her hideously ugly son, Morfran (later called Afagddu), by anointing him with the cauldron's potion. Alas, on the appointed day, the first three drops were spilled on the servant, Gwion, as he stirred the pot, giving him the wisdom and inspiration intended for Morfran. An enraged Cerridwen chased after Gwion. Both shapeshifted into various animal forms, until Gwion, having finally morphed into a grain of corn, was eaten by Cerridwen, who had now transformed into a hen. Powered by the potion, Gwion lived within Cerridwen and entered the body of her next born son. Unwilling to kill her baby, Cerridwen threw him into the sea in a basket, where he was rescued by a Welsh prince. He named the baby Taliesin, who grew up to be the legendary Welsh poet.

Taliesin means "shining brow." Wright first used Taliesin as the name for his home in Wisconsin, which was built on the brow of a hill. Wright believed that architecture developed and evolved from folk legend and myth. He liked the idea of rebirth and a new start that the abandoned son of Cerridwen received when he was found and given the name, Taliesin.

On a recent Thanksgiving, Lori and I explored Taliesin West with my sister, Karen, who lives in the Phoenix area. As we drove into the homestead, Taliesin West seemed to emerge from and integrate with the desert landscape around it. Walking through the complex of structures, we sensed that Wright incorporated Native American tradition and the desert landscape, along with his Welsh culture, when designing his works. Our intuition proved to be correct.

At Taliesin West, the Welsh myth is blended with the Native American past. When we had entered the property, we noticed a familiar-looking pattern within a square, on the gate. Sure enough, it was taken from a petroglyph Wright found on the property. The design depicted, through a series of interlocking straight lines, the concept of two hands clasping each other in friendship. The image brought to mind old Celtic traditions of a similar nature. One that Lori and I had reenacted in Ireland's Glencomcile recalled lovers touching or clasping their fingers or hands through the hole in a standing stone, signifying the permanence of their vows.

The square shape and geometric pattern also reminded us of a related design at the Wright-inspired Arizona Biltmore Hotel, where we had stayed during our prior year visit to Phoenix. The hotel's exterior walls featured rectangular blocks incorporating a modernistic rendering of a desert palm tree.

The connection with the desert and the earth was felt throughout our tour across the arid environs of Taliesin West. The home and connected drafting studio were built with a low lying profile of sloping walls, and prominent timbers separating the white roof sections; originally movable canvas sheets that gave the structure the look, when raised, of a ship sailing serenely across the desert, parallel to the nearby McDowell Mountains.

For walls, Wright developed "Organic Architecture," using the natural materials found in the immediate area, including sand, and quartzite rocks, to form "Desert Masonry." Wright was the first to use this technique. The solid strength exuded by the hard stone faces was reminiscent of the ancient Welsh portal tombs, whose rock walls were topped by huge limestone capstones.

Taliesin West is a self-contained compound, including apartments for students and colleagues, library, theatre, pools, dining and laundry areas. Broad terraces and walkways connect the diverse components. A Master's architectural school is still operational, alternating by season with the Wisconsin Taliesin site.

Returning that evening to our hotel, the Sheraton Wild Horse Pass in Chandler, we experienced the blending of local folklore with the desert landscape there as well. The hotel, an expansive low-lying structure spreading across the Sonoran desert landscape, is owned by the Pima and Maricopa Tribes and is situated on their Gila River Indian Reservation. The hotel applies the principles of "geotourism" to guide its operations. According to National Geographic, geotourism is defined as tourism that sustains or enhances the geographical character of a place—its environment, culture, aesthetics, heritage, and the well-being of its residents. Wright would have been proud.

For us, the shining gem that exemplified most brightly this dedication to cultural sustainability, was the hotel's Kai Restaurant. The only five star restaurant in Arizona, Kai exuded Southwestern elegance and culture from the moment we walked in. When greeting us, our waiter, after alerting us not to be alarmed, proceeded to welcome us using the Pima language. Then he presented the menus, each covered with Native Artwork depicting a different tribal story. Before explaining the menu items, he shared an age-old story from one of the pictures that displayed fish swimming past desert figures.

The menu sections were titled "The Birth," "The Beginning," "The Journey," and "The Afterlife," to represent the different courses. While here symbolizing aspects of local culture, they parallel universal myths of the life cycle. Even the restaurant's name, Kai, is Pima for "seed."

Kai also prides itself on serving dishes prepared with locally farmed ingredients, such as mesquite smoked pumpkin soup and hand-picked lettuces. Among the creatively presented entrees were tenderloin of tribal buffalo and high country elk loin. Typical of the special touches, sorbet was served between courses in an eggshell shaped dish set upon a nest of woven twigs.

Kai Restaurant and the Wild Horse Pass enhanced the perspective we had experienced that day at Taliesin West. Returning to our room that evening surrounded by the quiet serenity of the desert, we felt at one with these two cultures, Welsh and Native American, as diverse, yet at the same time sharing a commonality that transcends all of humankind.

Lake Near Skoki Lodge

Skoki Lodge

Chapter 22
Splendor and Solitude in the Canadian Rockies

The relaxed enchantment of Skoki Lodge

Unless you're a prince or princess, reaching Skoki Lodge requires a challenging, yet inspiring hike of seven miles. Nestled high among the Canadian Rockies in Banff National Park, the lodge and its surroundings have offered solitude and breathtaking natural vistas to hearty travelers since 1931.

Just days before a trek to Skoki, I had hiked to a waterfall in Johnston Canyon, located on the popular Bow Valley Parkway, just a few miles south of the Skoki trailhead. Though skies were overcast and rainy, hundreds of park visitors descended on the limestone-walled canyon, often impatient with the pace of others on the narrow walkway. Normally an enchanting diversion, the gridlocked gorge was now a victim of its own allure and accessibility.

I observed a similar result a few miles north at Lake Louise, where I spent the night at the renowned Chateau before striking out for Skoki. The stunning uniqueness of the lake, whose turquoise waters shimmer, gemlike within a setting of sheer, glacier-clad peaks, was dulled by the daily horde of 16,000 partakers, crowding in for a look. The broad lakeside path became a congested freeway of humanity, with anxious vacationers darting and weaving as they went.

By now I knew that any chance of gaining even a hint of the tranquility and solitude the early explorers sensed, would first entail an extended hike on a mountain trail, leaving comforts and crowds behind. That was reason enough. On a sunny August morning, seven colleagues and I set out. Once on the trail, we spotted a grizzly bear, deer and several hoary marmots, but only a handful of humans. Nevertheless, each new turn in our path revealed yet more spectacular vistas, evoking spontaneous wow's from group members.

Crossing Boulder and Deception Passes gave us a thousand foot elevation gain prior to reaching Skoki. Along the way, snow-speckled peaks with names like Wall of Jericho and Fossil Mountain mesmerized our senses, as did the emerald green lakes with their glacial fed streams and waterfalls. Wildflowers of yellow, blue, lavender, white and red covered the alpine meadows.

At Skoki, a friendly staff from Australia and New Zealand greeted us warmly, with lemonade and an array of cheese, crackers, pumpkin bread and cheesecake. At dinner, we met Leo Mitzel, the manager of ten years, who shared the Skoki spirit with us. Raised in a family that led horseback tours in the area, Leo exuded the mellow lifestyle that typified the Skoki legacy.

Leo related the story of Prince William, son of the Prince of Wales, and Princess Catherine, Duchess of Cambridge, who he and his wife, Katie, hosted on the royals' honeymoon trip in 2011. Though protocol required running water and toilet facilities, features non-existent before and after the visit, Leo sensed that

England's future king and queen would have been just as happy without.

The next morning as we shared a cup of coffee by the fire before others arose, Leo asked me: "You're from Chicago. Why do you come to places like this?" I responded: "I feel closer to God here. It's a spiritual experience for me." Leo replied that it was spiritual for him as well. When he needed spiritual help, he told me he climbed to a mountain top, where he felt God's presence. He didn't need organized religion.

Leo enjoyed meeting guests with the diverse backgrounds that arrive at Skoki from all corners of the world. He observed that usually the hike in to Skoki changed peoples' perspective. Having endured the exhausting hike myself the prior day, I could relate to what he was saying. The effort tended to show the commonality of our human limitations, resulting in a relaxed atmosphere where mutual respect flowed effortlessly.

Following breakfast, Leo sat at our table with a folder of maps and a marker, to lay out the day's hikes for us. We selected Merlin Lake, which the royal couple had tackled on their visit. After marking the way, Leo handed the map to me, "Here, this is yours. Use it to guide the way."

On the trail an hour later, I had developed a new found respect for the pluck of the Prince and Princess. A boulder field and steep rocky scramble near the top caused some anxious moments. Hand holds in narrow crevices for lifting, coordinated with careful foot placement, were called for to negotiate the final few steps.

The brotherly perspective Leo had mentioned became apparent, when my hiking companion and I noticed a woman afraid to proceed. "Let us help. You can make it," I said. Though we were strangers, she willingly trusted our guidance and outstretched hands to bring her through the most precarious section. At this moment, we were fellow seekers on a common journey.

The demanding effort proved worthwhile when, at the top we viewed the placid grandeur of Merlin Lake filling the valley below us. A restful lunch at the serene lakeshore followed, beneath the purview of a hoary marmot peering boldly from atop a nearby boulder.

The longer we stayed at Skoki the closer the bond grew with the other guests at the lodge, who came to feel more like family. There was no other choice, since we found ourselves in the back country together, in close quarters with nowhere else to go. Happily, Skoki has welcomed no more than 24 guests at a time since opening in 1931, a far cry from the crowds down below.

We all gathered around two tables to feast on the cuisine, which displayed a level of sophistication not expected with accommodations that lacked running water or electricity. The dinner menu boasted New Zealand lamb, organic rice & quinoa, roasted beets, corn medley and apple caramel cake. Second helpings were welcome and taken gladly. Dining in candlelight transformed the atmosphere of the rustic room into that of a secluded romantic hideaway.

The scenic splendor of the area coupled with the gracious ambiance, softened the harsh realities of existence taken for granted back home. Crave a shower? A bowl of warm water and a rag will have to do. Feet sore from hiking over rough terrain? Soothe them in the cold, rushing water of the nearby stream. Need to answer nature's call during the night? Bundle up and grab a flashlight before venturing to the outhouse a dozen steps away from the lodge.

Did you bring a good book to wile away the quiet hours? The gift of time was my most cherished gift at Skoki. Though modern daily life has a way of consuming every moment, up there unfettered time flowed abundantly: early in the morning, after a day hike, and in the evening hours. Some napped, while others enjoyed games. I prized the freedom to just sit and contemplate; to reflect; to find myself.

The prince and princess chose Skoki Lodge as a honeymoon stop for two reasons: its remoteness and its reputation for friendly hospitality. Having been the benefactor of Leo and the staff's care and kindness, I am confident the royal couple were not disappointed in that regard. Even so, with the constant exposure that defines their existence, I can only hope that the special quality of Skoki's remoteness brought a brief taste of the solitude they sought.

PLAYBILL®

ST. JAMES THEATRE

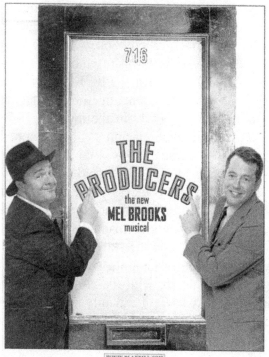

Chapter 23

Springtime for Broadway

A poignant birthday foray to New York

Note: This chapter still resonates as a wistful memory for me. Flying across country on an airliner to New York City, in the spring of 2001, was a final journey in what now seems like the age of innocence prior to 9/11.

New York seemed like a long way to go just to see a show. Los Angeles has a robust theatre scene itself. How much better can a production like *The Lion King,* at the vintage *Pantages T*heatre, be in New York?

But this was different. Mel Brooks' *The Producers* had just made an historic opening on Broadway, sweeping up a record twelve Tony awards. I already had an excuse to head east, since my niece was getting married in Chicago. Why not make an extra stop in The Big Apple? Besides, it was my birthday.

My wife, Lori, who normally hates to travel, was suspiciously receptive, until she finally confessed, "My favorite group, The Irish Tenors, has a date at Radio City Music Hall the same weekend." Put it altogether, plus the good fortune of snagging a couple of *The Producers* tickets for $90 each on the internet, before they became impossible to get, and we were off to LAX at 5:30 AM on June 20.

With our 8 AM flight scheduled to arrive in New York at 4:36 PM, there was little room for error in order to make *The Producers* 8 PM curtain that evening. The fact that this flight had been cancelled a couple times the prior week motivated our early arrival at the airport in hopes of catching an earlier departure. Racing to the gate at 6:45, we luckily made the 7 AM flight. At the ticket counter, a smiling ten year old girl helped her mother issue the boarding passes. Moments later on board, her sweet young voice brought a cheerful welcome over the intercom, as we collapsed into our seats.

Five hours and three time zones later, we landed at JFK airport. Another forty-five minutes in a taxi brought us to the Waldorf Astoria Hotel by 4:30 PM. Having prepared for a late arrival and a rush to the theatre, we now marveled that there would actually be time to freshen up and have dinner before the show.

More relaxed now, we settled into the Hotel's highly rated Peacock Alley Restaurant. The rich wood paneling, peacock mural and quiet ambience were a welcome respite from our hurried travels and the frenetic New York City pace outside. General Manager Hagen Freihoff took time to welcome us and review the unusual menu. "There are no individual prices. One to seven courses can be ordered, with pricing per number of courses, regardless of which dishes are chosen." Lori picked the Copper River salmon preceded by asparagus with morel mushrooms. I had grouper, Asian style, in a soy sauce, with a lobster broth starter. Both were wonderful. But the reality of being in New York hit home when we got the check. Our two course meals were $44 each. Add to this $10 for a bottle of water, $5 coffees, and a single glass of wine and dessert between us, and our final tab plus tip was a Gothamesque $167.

Patting our well fed stomachs, we stepped into the lobby at 7:15 PM and asked the concierge for directions to the theatre. "The St. James is a good fifteen minute walk," he noted. We opted instead for a taxi to get us there with ample time to spare. Little did we know that a flight from LA is more predictable than navigating a few blocks across New York City in a car. Manhattan is one place where driving can take twice as long as walking.

We sat in the taxi, sweating, in barely moving traffic, which consisted mainly of other taxis. After thirty minutes, when we were just about to leap from the cab to make a run for it, *The Producers* marquee finally appeared. We joined the throngs of excited theatergoers, crowding into the St. James, ten minutes before curtain. Various patrons were congratulating each other on their good luck in acquiring the much sought after tickets. A stairway led to our seats in the mezzanine of the seasoned old theatre.

Our efforts and anticipation were rewarded when Nathan Lane, Matthew Broderick and the rest of the cast began the delightful farce. *The Producers* is based on the 1968 movie of the same name that won Mel Brooks an Academy Award. As a CPA, I especially enjoyed Broderick's Leo Bloom, a down-trodden accountant who goes astray chasing his fantasy after finding his client, Lane's Max Bialystock, cooking the books. Their sure fire scheme to pocket millions by intentionally staging a flop goes comically awry when their play, *Springtime for Hitler*, becomes a smash hit, landing them in Sing Sing Prison.

The musical combined lavish sets and costumes, hummable melodies, superb acting, and an outrageously funny script that offends almost everyone. The audience reaction brought an instant standing ovation at the finish.

Broadway was abuzz with theatergoers piling out of various shows as we walked back to the hotel. With huge Time Square signs lit up and flashing like Las Vegas, there was obviously no power shortage in New York.

The next morning called for a leisurely breakfast in bed, so we ordered room service in the spacious mini-suite that ran a mere $10 over the regular room rate of $269. Classically furnished, featuring a comfortable king bed and sofa, the suite offered his and her closets on either end. The view from the several tall windows was primarily of the other wing of the forty-two floor hotel, with a glimpse of Park Avenue below. The healthful bowls of oatmeal we ordered came with raisins, brown sugar and an unhealthy bill for $32, tip already included. At least the in-room coffee service was complementary.

Fed and rested, we descended to the main floor at 11 AM. The grandeur of a prior era was resplendently present at the Waldorf. An ornately sculpted nine foot high bronze and mahogany clock designed for the 1893 Chicago World's Fair, adorns the center of the large main lobby. Reception lined one side of the bustling, sofa filled room, with the entrance to Peacock Alley restaurant and lounge at the other side. The restaurant name originated from the strutting of the fashionably dressed society ladies down the elegant hallway to the Park Avenue Lobby during the early part of the century. Strolling in that direction, we paused to admire the 148,000 piece mosaic in the floor depicting the Wheel of Life by French artist, Louis Rigal.

Looking forward to the concert that evening, we left the hotel and walked several blocks to Radio City Music Hall for the Back Stage Tour. Part of the Rockefeller Center complex of buildings, the theatre was built in 1932 to pair up movies with vaudeville performances. The 5,000 seat auditorium premiered such classics as *Gone With the Wind*. Of course, the Music Hall's most famous occupants today are the Rockettes. We caught a brief glimpse of the dance troupe rehearsing a new production, Carnivalle, for next year. Their quick, animated movements left no doubt as to the tough conditioning required to perform the intricate numbers. As we moved through the art deco foyer, Lori gave me a knowing grin when we overheard a fellow tour member lament: "We wanted to see *The Producers*, but the scalper wanted $1,500."

After the tour, we dodged intermittent rainfall on the way back to the hotel. Once there, Lori napped, while I located the hotel's business center to catch up on my email. In the evening we dined at Tuscan Square, an Italian eatery we had spotted near the theatre that afternoon. We both had the mixed grill, consisting of lamb chops, veal scaloppini and chicken breast. I started with a green salad, while Lori tried the tomato and bread soup, tasty but rich and more like a pudding.

Once at Radio City Music Hall, Lori met up with fellow Irish Tenor fans she had gotten to know through an internet fan group. The acquaintance paid off as one of them had arranged for our eighth row center seats in the cavernous auditorium.

The Irish Tenors, Finbar Wright, Anthony Kearns, and Ronan Tynan, were in fine form that night. Their jovial banter and rich, lyrical voices made the 2-1/2 hour performance a delight. The concert was part of their Ellis Island Tour, based on their televised PBS special concert at the historic site where millions of immigrants entered the United States, from 1892 to 1943. They sang numerous traditional Irish songs, along with such favorites as "How are Things in Gloccamorra," "Danny Boy," and the beautiful Johnnie Cash tune, "Forty Shades of Green." By the close of the show, everyone was on their feet, as the Tenors led an unforgettable "God Bless America," while a huge American flag descended to the stage. The standing ovation continued exuberantly until they rewarded the enthusiastic audience with several encores.

The next morning, pleased with our quick, theatre filled escape to New York, we flew to Chicago for my niece, Lisa's wedding, also a spectacular production. But that's another story.

London Bridge Over Lake Havasu

Village at Lake Havasu

Chapter 24
Merry Old Lake Havasu
London Bridge is all lit up

For years my wife, Lori, and I have used the Thanksgiving weekend as a time to explore different parts of Arizona with my sister, Karen, who lives in Phoenix. Having covered all the major sights, we wondered what we could do this time. After I took a close look at the map, I remarked to Lori, "It should be obvious. We've vacationed in far off England several times, but we've never even seen the London Bridge in nearby Lake Havasu City."

Transported across the sea in pieces by the McCulloch Oil Corporation in 1968, London Bridge became the focal point for a new planned community on the shores of the lake formed by Parker Dam, on the Colorado River.

Departing on Wednesday morning to beat the rush out of town from Santa Ana, California, we quickly traversed the desert, arriving in Lake Havasu City five hours later. Spotting London Bridge for the first time, however, was easier than crossing it. Wisely, there is no direct access from State Highway 95. After several wrong turns, we found McCulloch Boulevard, the street that transits the Bridge.

Named after the city's founder, the boulevard continues onto the island created when the Bridge was erected. As we crossed, I envisioned ornate, horse-drawn carriages of old, led by drivers in Beefeater regalia. In reality, the Bridge now is primarily a means for modern folk like us to get to the island resorts.

A mile further, our destination, Nautical Inn, appeared. Situated on a scenic cove looking out toward the City and Bridge, the Inn features 120 rooms, suites and two-bedroom condos. Lori and I settled into a first floor parlor suite, plain but clean, with a sofa, two double beds, and a broad picture window of the style found on a ship. Our suite was just steps from the beach that formed a small horseshoe shape around to the restaurant and rental boat dock across the way. As we approached our suite, several quacking ducks started following, correctly judging us as good prospects for a handout. Lori broke out a package of cookies, appropriately imported from England, much to the satisfaction of the growing throng of birds.

Before long, we headed further down the road to the Beachcomber RV Park to meet Karen, with her motorhome and pets, Lucky, a Weimaraner dog, and cats, Tiger and Pumpkin. After an enthusiastic welcome from all, we were ready to seek out the English Village for some dinner. Located at the foot of London Bridge, the quaint buildings and shops give a glimpse of Merry Old England. London Arms Pub and Brewery, formerly owned by Brits, seemed a fitting spot for some good British beer and cuisine. We were not disappointed. With several ales, stouts and lagers to choose from, we picked raspberry ale. The ale went well with the authentic bangers and mash, accompanied by mushy peas and oxtail soup. Our waiter quipped that the sound of oxtail scares some folks, so he usually describes the soup as beef barley.

A walk around the shops was needed following the hearty meal. Christmas lights were going up all around, in anticipation of the lighting ceremony to come on Friday.

Thanksgiving Day began bright and sunny, with a slight chill in the air. A leisurely morning watching powerboats, kayaks and a seaplane pull up on our beach preceded the holiday meal at noon. Karen joined us at the Captain's Table Restaurant, a short stroll around the beach from our suite. Our window-side table provided an expansive view of the lake, from the mountains off in the East to London Bridge in the West.

Karen and I feasted on a traditional turkey dinner with all the trimmings, while Lori savored a succulent roast duck with plum sauce. Curried pumpkin bisque started the meal and homemade pumpkin pie topped it off.

Stuffed to the gills from the delicious meal, some more walking was in order. We started in London Bridge Park, across the lake from the English Village, then drove over to Rotary Community Park on the other side of the lake. Finally a ten-minute drive brought us to Cattail Cove, a favorite RV camping and hiking spot south of the city.

Later, in the lounge of the Nautical Inn, some dark beer and chicken quesidillas finished off the evening, accompanied by a Faith Hill concert on the bar TV.

On Friday, the time came to sample what the lake had to offer. While families were loading up houseboats, wave runners and other craft, we opted for the cushy, air-conditioned comfort of the Bluewater Jetboat Tour. Before boarding, we lunched at an outdoor patio next to London Bridge. Amidst the historic splendor, we were entertained with the chatter of workmen diligently putting the finishing touches on the Christmas lights for tonight's ceremony. They had competition from barkers for the Dixie Bell riverboat and Kon Tiki, also hawking lake tours.

Departing from the foot of London Bridge after lunch, the jetboat soon whisked us north along the Havasu National Wildlife Refuge. We were disappointed not to spot any wild burros left over from the mining days. But graceful egrets, predatory hawks, and a young bald eagle attacking a seagull drew our attention.

The dramatic, red-rock Topock gorge was the highlight. The boat captain piqued our imaginations, pointing out rock formations with names like Sleeping Indian, Stargazer, Scorpion, Dolphin, Auto and Dolly Parton Rocks. On one large rock face, several large, ancient Indian petroglyphs were visible from the boat, depicting birds, the sun and strange creatures.

The boat trip covered forty miles in 2-1/2 hours. Disembarking, there was just time for a snack before the lighting ceremony at 6 PM. Returning to the London Arms Pub and Brewery, we munched on scotch eggs (hardboiled eggs encased in sausage and deep-fried) and arti-poppers (artichoke hearts in puff pastry), washed down with dark stout and hard cider.

As six o'clock approached, crowds started to gather on the waterfront in the English Village. We clamored up the stairs to the top of London Bridge for a strategic vantage point from which to take in the festivities. The tradition in Lake Havasu City is for hearty swimmers to race across the channel on this night each year. The route along the bridge covers 300 yards in cold, Colorado River water. After a last minute delay in the chilly night air, the race of about fifteen swimmers got underway to the cheers of the crowd. The winner, in addition to some monetary prizes and bragging rights, earned the honor of flipping an enormous switch that turned on the holiday lights in the whole Village and Bridge area.

Accompanied by much hoopla and fanfare, the moment finally came. All at once the darkened Village was aglow with thousands of colored lights. Each building and tree was swathed in a different color, giving the glittering effect reminiscent of the Disneyland Main Street Electrical Parade. Even London Bridge was tastefully decorated with huge lighted wreaths on each span and many a glowing lamppost. Duly launched, the Festival of Lights would continue through January 7, along with a Boat Parade of Lights on December 2.

Having stood on the cold granite Bridge for over an hour, we were ready to warm up with a hot drink and supper. We walked the rest of the way to the far side of the bridge, hoping the restaurants there would be less crowded. Shugrues only required a half-hour wait, and the view across the channel from its waterfront perch made the twinkling lighted Village appear like a fairyland. Satiated from seemingly continuous eating, we opted for the seafood Caesar salads, which came full of shrimp and crab.

The next morning, realizing this taste of England in the desert would have to hold us until our next trip abroad, we bid farewell to Karen and the pets, and headed home to California, ready for the holidays to come.

Epilogue

My Celtic Journey comes to a close, for now. Fittingly, what started with Christmas in Ireland, has now been completed with a Christmas celebration on London Bridge. The uniqueness of Celtic Spirituality has flowed evocatively throughout my travels, providing a window to the extraordinary world of the Celtic people across the ages. The richness of the tradition and legend have shaped their ongoing search toward meaning, much like we each are shaped by the past and the experiences on our own personal journey.

May all our journeys endure and continue to broaden our vision. For as the proverb of old proclaims: "the journey is the reward."

If you have enjoyed this book, please consider posting a review on Amazon.com, Goodreads, and other review sites. The author may be reached through the website www.gaeltales.com.

Appendix A

The Loves of Lori

A tribute to the author's source of inspiration

The occasion was a dinner party in the quiet back room at Zov's Restaurant in Tustin, California. A dozen guests were seated around a large banquet table. They had just finished their meal when a melodic voice rang out.

"You made me love you. I didn't want to do it. I didn't want to do it."

Lori's friend captured everyone's attention, as she rose from her chair singing. The party was in honor of Lori's birthday. The words her friend sang, at my secret request, hearkened back to a young Judy Garland, singing to a photo of Clark Gable.

So began the sentimental tribute to "The Loves of Lori." But for me it was a tale of surrender to an inevitable "truth universally acknowledged" (with apologies to Jane Austen):

If you're contemplating a relationship with a writer of romance, be forewarned. You may find yourself in futile competition with a string of popular heart throbs.

But how was I to know that the first time I saw her decades ago, smiling across a crowded room? I hadn't been there when a young Lori identified herself with Garland's singing her heart out to Gable's image. Any yearnings that may have been stirring on the enchanted evening when we met, were hidden within her creative mind.

"Gigi, have I been standing up too close or back too far?"

This time a rich tenor voice filled the room of birthday well-wishers.

An early date should have given me a clue of what was to come. Lori asked to see French actor, Louis Jourdan, in Noel Coward's play, *Private Lives*. The play was innocent enough, but afterwards, when we spotted Jourdan at a nearby restaurant, Lori couldn't tear herself away from the window, admiring him from afar. Later she confessed that she dreamed of herself as the Gigi that Jourdan wooed in the award winning film.

"Soldier boy. O my little soldier boy. I'll be true to you."

A feminine voice serenaded in the innocent style of the Shirelles. By now the fun loving dinner guests were catching on.

In the early years, I was the confident, clueless war veteran. Back from Viet Nam, I moved to the north side of Chicago. After months taking in the scene at nearby pubs, I accepted a friend's invitation to a singles group at a gothic church on Michigan Avenue.

There one Sunday evening I saw her. Lori was talking to another girl. Her irresistible smile and easy laugh held my gaze. With a knowing look, my friend introduced us.

Lori won me over with exotic terms like ZPG (zero population growth), convincing me that beyond her sweet demeanor was a thoughtful person with deeply held values. She too was won over, by accounts of my army service and my photos in uniform. Who could top that? Little did I know.

For us, it was love at first sight. A year later, we married. After several blissful years, we moved to California, where it all began. Having left family and friends, Lori had time on her hands. She began to write. She had told me that she enjoyed watching old romantic movies. If she didn't like the way one ended, she rewrote it in her mind.

Before long a New York editor called, extolling her first work. The title, NO TIME FOR LOVE, was fitting for a romance whose hero resembled the unreachable concertmaster in her high school orchestra. Impressed with her early success, I didn't realize what was happening.

"I am your angel of music."

At the birthday dinner, a sheepish smile crept over the face of Lori's friend, Dana, when a deep voice mouthed those mysterious words.

We had heard of *The Phantom of the Opera*, when it swept to meteoric success. Having always loved musicals, we went to see it with Dana and her husband in Los Angeles. By the end of the first act, the ladies were literally palpitating over the Tony-winning leading man's sensual performance. I finally realized that Lori's beloved soldier boy faced serious competition from a phantom named Michael Crawford.

Over the next two years, Lori saw *The Phantom of the Opera* dozens of times. Dana, an Olympic swimming medal winner, wrote to Crawford asking for a meeting. That scored her and Lori a private backstage encounter. It was no surprise when Lori's groundbreaking OBSESSION vampire novel series featured a character suspiciously like Crawford, her angel of music.

"Mucushla, Mucushla, your sweet voice is calling."

This time, I tried to invoke Lori's next heart throb, as I sang one of his sorrowful Irish songs, rather weakly.

Things got worse years later, after Crawford left, and Lori's passionate memories faded. A PBS special introduced The Irish Tenors. I could tell trouble was brewing, with the way she looked at the young tenor of the group: Anthony Kearns.

The next few years found us crisscrossing the states following his concerts. The original inspiration for Lori's creative Irish works of women's fiction, Kearns evoked comparisons to legendary Irish tenor John McCormack.

Lori became an obsessed fan. A research trip for her latest novel, THE THIN PLACE, spanned all of Ireland, complete with Irish Tenors concerts in Killarney, Belfast, and Dublin. I had gone from adored soldier boy to dependable tour guide. But I wouldn't admit that the music struck a chord in my own Irish heritage.

The party was winding down. As they departed, guests merrily signed greetings on a poster of photos recapping the "Loves of Lori."

Months later, I could only guess what further humiliation waited as I eyed a wrapped gift. It was addressed to "My Hero." Was there yet another one? Lori urged me to open it. As I did, a framed photograph emerged, depicting a handsome young soldier in Viet Nam. With renewed confidence, I recalled that distant place and my "selfie" so long ago.

Looking up, I met Lori's loving smile. Despite the numerous fantasies her romantic mind had conjured up over forty years of marriage, her soldier boy remained first in her heart.

Then she asked coyly: "Dmitri Hvorostovsky, the Russian opera star we saw in *Eugene Onegin* is coming to Los Angeles for a concert. Wanna go?"

Appendix B
A Sampling of the Author's Favorite Places
Ireland Highlights

1. Dublin

Hotels

Westbury – on Grafton Street- a classy hotel on a popular, pedestrian only shopping street. (http://www.doylecollection.com/hotels/the-westbury-hotel)

Shelburne – on St Stephen's Green-a classy historic hotel across from the park.

(https://www.theshelbourne.com/)

Top Sights

Guinness Storehouse –brewery tour.

Trinity College – historic Book of Kells (ornate Bible from 6th century).

Other lesser sights - Dublin Castle, St. Patrick's Cathedral, Jameson Distillery, Kilmainham Gaol, and Temple Bar.

Near Dublin South

Glendalough – in Wicklow Mountains, historic abbey ruins set between two lakes.

There is a moderately priced hotel on the grounds.
(http://www.glendaloughhotel.com/)

Near Dublin-North

Newgrange – 5,000 year old passage tombs (Ireland's pyramids).

Rossnaree-a favorite historic B & B in view of Newgrange. (http://www.rossnaree.ie/)

Itinerary

Fly in to Dublin and stay 3-4 nights at the Westbury. On the first day tour the Guinness Storehouse and Trinity College, or take a city tour. On the second day drive or take a tour to Glendalough. On the third day, drive or take a tour to Newgrange.

2. Southern Ireland

Killarney-beautiful lakes.

Park Hotel Kenmare-a favorite hotel in a quaint village. We spent Christmas there.

(http://www.parkkenmare.com/index.php)

Ring of Kerry – scenic peninsula. Also, Beara peninsula is there.

Kinsale – pretty port city with fort near Cork.

Ballymaloe House B&B-near Kinsale- has a cooking school (http://www.ballymaloe.ie/)

Dingle peninsula-scenic peninsula.

Cliffs of Moher, County Clare-scenic high cliffs.

Bunratty Castle & Folk Park-near Shannon.

Dromoland Castle-a classy hotel.
(http://www.dromoland.ie/)

Lesser sights-Blarney Castle, Burren.

Itinerary

Fly into Shannon, stay at Dromoland Castle and visit
Bunratty Castle & Folk Park. Next day drive to
Killarney, lakes and Ring of Kerry or Beara and stay
at Park Hotel Kenmare. Next day drive to Cork, visit
Blarney Castle, Kinsale and stay at Ballymaloe
House. Next day drive to visit Glendalough &
Wicklow Mountains, and arrive in Dublin. Stay at
Westbury Hotel on Grafton Street.

3. Northern Ireland

Giant's Causeway-scenic volcanic sight at the
northern tip of the country (like Devil's Postpile in
CA).

Carrick-a-Rede Rope Bridge-scenic walking bridge
near Causeway.

Bushmills Distillery-tour.

Whitepark House-a favorite B&B near Giant's
Causeway-host Bob was Landlady of the year.
(http://www.whiteparkhouse.com/)

Slieve League-highest sea cliffs in Europe, with
Glencolmcille Folk Village near by.

Castle Murray House-a favorite B&B in Dunkineely.
(http://www.castlemurray.com/)

Galway & Connemara peninsula.

Ashford Castle Hotel, Cong-a classy favorite (where The Quiet Man was filmed).

(http://www.ashfordcastle.com/)

Manor House Hotel-a favorite iconic hotel, with scenic setting on Lower Lough Erne.
(http://www.manorhousecountryhotel.com/)

Other sights – Belfast, Londonderry, Sligo.

<u>Itinerary</u>

From Dublin, drive to Newgrange and stay at Rossnaree House. Next day drive to Northern Coast to see Giant's Causeway and Carrick-a-Rede Rope Bridge. Stay at White Park House in Ballintoy. Next day drive to Enniskillen and stay at Manor House, Kildeas, on Lower Lough Erne. Next day drive back to Dublin.

There are many other castles and historic sites in Ireland, as well as scenic areas, gardens, cathedrals and museums.

Scotland Highlights, plus England and Wales

1. Edinburgh

Hotel

Balmoral – central Edinburgh next to train station. (https://www.roccofortehotels.com/hotels-and-resorts/the-balmoral-hotel/)

Top Sights

Edinburgh Castle.

Near Edinburgh

Stirling Castle – Braveheart country.

Rosslyn Chapel – where Da Vinci Code movie found the Holy Grail.

Further out

Loch Lomand – a pretty lake and scenery in the Trossachs.

Roman Camp Hotel-a nice B&B. (http://www.romancamphotel.co.uk/)

Loch Ness – legendary lake.

Loch Ness Lodge – a classy B&B overlooking Loch Ness. (http://www.loch-ness-lodge.com/)

Saint Andrews – birthplace of golf.

Isle of Iona – a favorite, but requires a drive across to west coast and 2 ferries – birthplace of Celtic Spirituality in the 6th century.

2. London

Hotels

The Savoy – our favorite in London, but pricy – half price rooms on Sunday.
(http://www.fairmont.com/savoy-london/)

Charing Cross Hotel (http://www.amba-hotel.com/hotels/united_kingdom/london/charing-cross/index.html) next to Charing Cross train station.

Both of these hotels are near the theatres.

Itinerary

Take the train from London to Edinburgh (about 4-1/2 hrs). Visit Edinburgh Castle and/or city tour. Stay at Balmoral Hotel. Next day drive to Stirling Castle, then on to Loch Lomand. Stay at Roman Camp Hotel. Next day drive to Loch Ness. Stay at Loch Ness Lodge. Next day drive back to Edinburgh, possibly stop at St. Andrews if interested in golf.

3. Lake District – northwest England – scenic lakes and rolling hills.

Sharrow Bay Country House Hotel – a classy small hotel tucked away on Ullswater.
(https://en.wikipedia.org/wiki/Sharrow_Bay_Country_House)

4. Cotswolds – quaint area in western England.

Swan Hotel, Bibury.
(http://www.cotswoldsfinesthotels.com/hotels-at-a-glance/the-swan-hotel-bibury.aspx)

5. Stonehenge – famous Neolithic monument in the south of England.

6. Wales

Tan-y-Foel Country House – a charming B & B near Betwys-y-Coed in the mountains of Snowdonia.

(http://www.tyfhotel.co.uk/)

Ramsey House – another charming B & B in St. Davids on the western coast of Wales.

(http://www.ramseyhouse.co.uk/)

There are many other castles and historic sites in Scotland, England & Wales, as well as scenic areas, gardens, cathedrals and museums.

About the Author

Gerald Herter grew up in the suburbs of Chicago, Illinois, graduated from the University of Wisconsin with BBA and MBA degrees in accounting, and achieved the status of Certified Public Accountant. He served in the United States Army as a field artillery officer in Germany and Viet Nam, and then worked for several years at Arthur Andersen & Company in Chicago.

Gerald met and married his wife, Lori, in the Chicago area. They moved to Southern California several decades ago, where he became associated with what would become HMWC CPAs & Business Advisors. He served as Managing Partner for many years, as well as President of the Americas, Asia & Australia Region of Integra International, a world-wide association of accounting firms. He also wrote and edited Integra's Audit & Accounting Alert newsletter for several years, and was a Contributing Editor for Accounting Technology magazine.

Gerald and Lori still live in Southern California with their cat, Marigold. They are long time members of Tustin Presbyterian Church, where Gerald serves as an elder. He also serves on the Boards of Directors of Family Promise of Orange County, a homeless shelter, and New Theological Seminary of the West.

Gerald and Lori have traveled extensively in the U.S., Canada, Europe, New Zealand, Australia, and Tahiti. Gerald has had travel articles published in the

New York Times, Chicago Tribune, Los Angeles Times, and Celtic Life International magazine.

Now that you have shared in the journeys to the Celtic world, you are ready for:

THE THIN PLACE
by Lori Herter

A travel writer flies to Ireland to explore sacred places cherished by her lost love, in hopes of finding new meaning in her life. But her intrusive and cagey co-author can't work without her. He follows, disturbing her spiritual journey as they visit mystical places and meet a mysterious femme fatale. Her lost love reappears and a long kept secret is revealed.

The Thin Place is available in print and as an eBook at Amazon.com and loriherter.com